Gigi

A Comedy in Two Acts

Dramatized by Anita Loos
(From the Novel by Colette)

A SAMUEL FRENCH ACTING EDITION

SAMUEL FRENCH

FOUNDED 1830

New York Hollywood London Toronto

SAMUELFRENCH.COM

GIGI

(2 males; 5 females)

STORY OF THE PLAY

Gigi is a young French girl brought up by her mother, grandmother and aunt to be a stylish cocotte. The man they have picked for her is a roue who frequently visits Gigi's home as a friend. When he comes, he brings her candy and lets her cheat him at cards. He is captivated by her boyish enthusiasm. But Gigi is now 16 and the time is ripe for her to put away the things of a child and to think of becoming the roue's mistress. But Gigi has not been brought up right; she doesn't think she would like such an arrangement. So in her own way, and much to the surprise of everyone, she maneuvers the roue into a proposition of marriage. This is treachery to the ladies, but Gigi thinks it is swell. "It brightens a playgoer's season considerably."—*Daily News*. "So much charm in its basic conceit . . . A gay little trinket."—*Herald Tribune*.

3

GIGI

Comedy by Anita Loos, adapted from Colette's novel: staged by Raymond Rouleau; settings by Raymond Sovey; presented by Gilbert Miller at the Fulton Theatre, November 24, 1951. The cast:

GIGI	*Audrey Hepburn*
MME. ALVAREZ	*Josephine Brown*
ANDREE	*Doris Patston*
GASTON LACHAILLE	*Michael Evans*
VICTOR	*Francis Compton*
ALICIA DE ST. EPHLAM	*Cathleen Nesbitt*
SIDONIE	*Bertha Belmore*

Synopsis: Paris, 1900

Act One

SCENE 1. *The apartment of Mme. Alvarez.*

SCENE 2. *The boudoir of Alicia de St. Ephiam.*

SCENE 3. *Mme. Alvarez's apartment.*

Act Two

SCENE 1. *Mme Alvarez's apartment.*

SCENE 2. *Alicia's boudoir.*

SCENE 3. *Mme. Alvarez's apartment.*

GIGI

CHARACTERS

(In the order of appearance)

GIGI
MME. ALVAREZ, *Gigi's grandmother*
ANDREE, *Gigi's mother*
GASTON LACHAILLE (TONTON)
VICTOR, *a butler*
ALICIA DE ST. EPHLAM
SIDONIE, *a maid*

Act One

Act Two

PLACE: *Paris—about 1900.*

Gigi

ACT ONE

Scene I

Time: *About 1900.*

Scene: *The modest living-room of Mme. Alvarez' apartment in Paris. There is a fireplace, down Right, with mantel, over which is a large mirror. (This mirror is of scrim, lighted and backed so as to give the effect of a mirror reflecting the objects on the mantel, as well as the room itself.) A lighted coal-stove fits under the mantel. There is a large arch at back, from Left to Right, draped with heavy red plush curtains, which opens into a dining-alcove and main entrance. A large window looks into the street from the Right wall of the dining alcove. Up Left Center a small arch or door leads into a tiny foyer, with front door to the apartment. A door in the up Left wall of the dining-alcove leads into the kitchen. And down Left (also heavily draped) is a door leading into the bedrooms and remainder of the apartment.*

The furnishings consist of a chair below the fireplace down Right; an armchair just Left of the fireplace; a straight chair above the fireplace. In the Center of the living-room is a low pouffe, a bit the worse for wear. An upright piano is against the

*Left wall, just above the bedroom door. A Victorian
sofa is at Left, so that there is a passage space between it and the piano. Just in front of the sofa,
about Left Center, is a small stand or table.*

*In the dining-alcove is a round dining-table
with a large red cover. Straight chair both Right
and Left of table. A buffet or side-board is against
the back (Right Center) wall of the alcove. A
wrought-iron clothes rack is in the foyer against
Left wall.*

*The apartment is heavy with pictures, mostly
photographs, of Andree at various stages of her
career, and a large picture of Gigi as a younger
child hangs over the piano.*

*A gas chandelier hangs over the dining-table; an
oil lamp is on the down stage end of mantel, and a
small gas fixture is on the Left wall of the foyer.
While the room is clean, there is a distinct feeling
of clutter and casual disorder.*

At Rise: Gigi *is seated at the piano doing her scale
exercises. From off in the bedroom comes the voice
of* Andree *doing her vocal exercises, which later
turns into the strains of the "Bell Song" from
"Lakme."*

Finally, the front door is opened by Mme. Alvarez, *the lady-of-the-house, an imposing woman
in her middle sixties. (In any sort of weather she
always sports a tan raincoat.) Over her arm is the
handle of her shopping bag, with a modest quantity
of provisions, including the inevitable long loaf of
bread.*

(Although born and bred in Paris, Mme. Alvarez *had long ago assumed the foreign name of a
departed lover and acquired a butter-like Spanish
paleness.)*

Mme. Alvarez. *(Looking about her as she enters;
calls out)* Gilberte! *(No answer. Louder)* Gilberte!

(Now MME. ALVAREZ *assumes a tone of reprimand)*
Gigi!

GIGI. *(Gives a start and turns)* Oh! What is it, Grandma?

MME. ALVAREZ *(Removing her coat)* You didn't hear me calling, when I came in just now?

GIGI. *(Crossing up to Left of her)* Why, no—Mama's making such a noise.

(At which point from off-stage come muffled strains of the "Bell Song," from "Lakme," practiced by someone with the all-too-professional technique of a hack singer.)

MME. ALVAREZ. Your mother's going to be late for her rehearsal.

GIGI. She isn't on till the second act. It's Frasquita.

MME. ALVAREZ. *(Giving* GIGI *her parcels)* Take these into the kitchen, and bring in the carrots.

*(*GIGI *does so, as* MME. ALVAREZ *takes coat and hat to hat-rack—then crosses down to curling-iron and papers on table front of sofa.)*

And don't forget you've got to go to your Aunt Alicia's.

GIGI. *(From kitchen)* Couldn't I go tomorrow, Grandma?

MME. ALVAREZ. *(Lighting alcohol stove)* Break an engagement with your Aunt?

GIGI. *(Returning from kitchen with carrots wrapped in piece of newspaper, paring-knife. She is chewing on a separate carrot.)* Well, couldn't I go without my hair being curled this time? *(Puts carrots and knife on table front of sofa.)*

MME. ALVAREZ. You could not! Sit there, on your stool.

*(*GIGI *complies, and, in order to sit on the stool, has to bend her long legs so that her skirt discloses her cotton stockings clear to the knees.* MME. ALVAREZ *glances at her legs, and takes three curl-papers, crosses to Left of* GIGI.*)*

Sometimes, when I look at those nice, long legs of yours, I regret that you never learned to dance.

GIGI. *(Chewing on carrot)* But I wanted to learn, Grandma. Why didn't you let me take lessons?

MME. ALVAREZ. *(Wrapping hair in curling-paper)* Your mother took lessons in singing—

(ANDREE's *voice sings a high note, which ends abruptly.)*

And look where she's ended up. Slaving away at the Opera Comique, and not even in principal roles.

(ANDREE *now sings a phrase of the "Bell Song.")*

GIGI. Do you think Maman will ever sing the Bell Song from Lakme, Grandma?

MME. ALVAREZ. Not where the public can hear her! *(Moves to Right of* GIGI, *applies another curl-paper.* ANDREE *gives five sharp, distorted vocal notes.)*

But I suppose there's no harm in her having her illusions. You see, my Gigi, lessons can give a girl ideas of a career. And a career is the ruination of any woman.

GIGI. Even of someone who gets to be famous?

MME. ALVAREZ. *(Applying third curling-paper)* For instance?

GIGI. Well—Polaire. Or Cleo de Merode.

MME. ALVAREZ. As if their careers were what made them famous!

GIGI. What was it, then?

MME. ALVAREZ. Never mind! *(Crosses to get curling-irons.)*

GIGI. You mean Polaire's a success because she's got a Russian Grand Duke. And Polaire a King?

MME. ALVAREZ. *(Correcting her)* "Mademoiselle" Polaire, and "Mademoiselle" de Merode. *(Twirling iron to cool it)* Try to show more respect for your betters, Gigi dear,—won't you? *(Tests iron on wrapping-paper.)*

GIGI. Yes, Grandma.

MME. ALVAREZ. *(Crossing to Left of* GIGI—*applying*

iron to her bangs) How often must I tell you to keep your knees together, when you're sitting on a stool?
(GIGI *obeys.)*
If you have to move, move them both, either to the right, or to the left.

GIGI. But I've got my drawers on, Grandma.

MME. ALVAREZ. Drawers are one thing, and decency is another. It's all in the point of view.

GIGI. But why couldn't my skirts be a little longer, Grandma?

MME. ALVAREZ. Really! And have you any other suggestions? *(Pats her cheek.)*

GIGI. *(With a show of spirit)* All you'd have to do would be to sew a little ruffle on the hems.

MME. ALVAREZ. And have your mother trailed around by a big horse, who'd look eighteen at least? With her job to think about? Use your head a little bit!

GIGI. I do! But with my skirts so short I always have to remember to bend my knees in the shape of a Z, on account of my "you-know-what."

MME. ALVAREZ. *(Shocked to the heart)* Gigi! Where did you ever hear such language?

GIGI. *(Matter-of-fact)* At school—one of the girls.

MME. ALVAREZ. Well, stay away from her!

GIGI. *(Docilely)* All right, Grandma. But what do you *call* it, then?

MME. ALVAREZ. *(A pause—then)* Nothing! It has no name.

(At which point GIGI'S *mother,* ANDREE, *enters through doorway leading off to bedrooms, humming and mechanically feeling her delicate tonsils.* ANDREE, *at 31, is faded and discouraged. She is wearing a faded negligee, and carries her shirtwaist. The other parts of her street clothes are draped on the Right dining-room chair. Her hat is on the mantel.)*

GIGI. *(At sight of her mother, gives a sudden exclamation)* OH!

MME. ALVAREZ. *(Long-suffering)* What now?

GIGI. *(Addressing* ANDREE*)* I forgot to get you the magazine you wanted, Mamma.

ANDREE. *(Exasperated)* Really, Gigi! *(Crossing front, to mantel, gets coin from her purse.)*

GIGI. *(To* MME. ALVAREZ*)* Couldn't I just run down to the kiosk now?

MME. ALVAREZ. *(Shocked)* In your curl-papers? *(Turns to* ANDREE*)* And what's so important about this magazine?

ANDREE. It's the latest *Theater Magazine*—they say there's a picture of me in it. *(Crosses; gives coin to* GIGI.*)*

MME. ALVAREZ. *(None too impressed)* I see!

ANDREE. *(Crosses and returns purse to mantel)* And the issue may all be gone, before I get one.

MME. ALVAREZ. *(Reluctant)* Oh, very well— *(To* GIGI*)* Run along!

*(*GIGI *rises, crosses to front door.)*

I'll take your curl-papers off when you get back. *(Calling after* GIGI*)* And pick up a copy of *Gil Blas* for me!

GIGI. I will! *(Exits.)*

*(*MME. ALVAREZ *blows out flame in alcohol-stove, and exits to kitchen for apron.)*

ANDREE. *(To her mother, amused)* You and your scandal magazine! *(Has removed her negligee, and is in bloomers and corsets. She puts foot on armchair Right and begins to adjust stockings and garters.)* Poor little monkey! She's so backward. Now, at her age, I was—

MME. ALVAREZ. *(Returning from kitchen, and tying her apron)* Don't throw roses at yourself for what you were at her age! *(To up Center)* If memory serves me right, at her age you threw over a rich flour magnate, to run away with a singing teacher!

ANDREE. Oh, let's not go into that now, Maman! *(Crossing to above chair, getting into position for* MME. ALVAREZ *to help her with corsets.)* —Please, Maman!

MME. ALVAREZ. *(Crossing to* ANDREE, *taking corset-*

strings and proceeding to tighten corsets) A singing
teacher—and when I think how that delightful old
gentleman, with flour mills all over the place, actually
hired the scoundrel— *(Presses her knee against* ANDREE,
in order to draw corset tighter.) Stop breathing— and
paid for the singing lessons!

ANDREE. Poor Georges—he wasn't really so bad at
heart, Maman.

MME. ALVAREZ. Not bad,—huh! *(Hands corset strings
to front of* ANDREE.)

ANDREE. But as soon as he found out he'd gotten me
into trouble, Georges wanted to— *(Tying corset-strings,
and going to chair to get remaining clothes.)*

MME. ALVAREZ. Wanted to marry you! *(Crossing to
sofa; sits and starts cleaning carrots)* Well, at least I
saved you from that dishonor. Are there any signs at
the theater that you're going to get the lead in this new
operetta?

ANDREE. *(Continues putting on clothes)* Oh, I'm sure
they'll give it to Tiphane. Everything goes to her. What
a life!

MME. ALVAREZ. Well, you chose it! Even so, you'd
be able to stand things better if you had an admirer
with a little dignity.

ANDREE. It's going to be hot today! *(Crossing down
to mantel; and puts on hat.)*

MME. ALVAREZ. You know what I'm talking about!

ANDREE. Yes, Maman! But you see I don't feel that
M. Durand is undignified. To be a clerk in a Post and
Telegraph office isn't such a bad career. At least, we can
look ahead to a pension.

MME. ALVAREZ. Oh, we can, eh? So you expect to
have him hanging around till then, do you?

ANDREE. *(Getting gloves and purse from mantel)* Is
it my fault, if I don't care for anyone else, Maman?

MME. ALVAREZ. It certainly is! It shows a complete
lack of self-control!

ANDREE. Oh well! *(A few steps to Center, putting on
gloves)* You know, Maman, if we only had a telephone,

I could have called up Leclerc and found out what was decided about the new operetta. Don't you think we should have one put in, Maman?—a telephone?

MME. ALVAREZ. I know why you want a telephone—-

ANDREE. (A few steps toward MME. ALVAREZ) If you think it's because—

MME. ALVAREZ. It's because you want to keep in touch with that no-account lover of yours!

ANDREE. But, Maman—

MME. ALVAREZ. A telephone is only useful to men who have big business-affairs, and women who have something to lie about. Now, if you'd get a lover with even a little money, I'd be the first to say "let's have a telephone,"—but as matters stand, we'll wait until Gigi is old enough to have an admirer.

ANDREE. (Crossing front of stool to up stage end of sofa) Admirer—poor Gigi! (Looking at picture over the piano) I wonder what her life is going to be! It's hard to tell even now what she'll look like. That nose of hers! Where did she ever get it?

MME. ALVAREZ. If you don't know, my child, who does?

GIGI. (At which point, GIGI comes bounding in with a copy of "Gil Blas" and "Le Theatre.") Here it is, Maman! (Handing them to her, skips up to sideboard, gets piece of licorice, humming a tune to herself.)

ANDREE. Thanks, dear. (Sits upper end sofa, looking through magazine.)

MME. ALVAREZ. (Crossing to above pouffe, with comb) Might as well look in the back of that—among the small pictures. Come, Gigi!

GIGI. (Crossing down and sitting on pouffe, as MME. ALVAREZ removes curl-papers) Grandma, couldn't you give me a little wave on the side for a change sometime?

MME. ALVAREZ. I certainly could not! To have your hair curl at the ends is as much eccentricity as a girl of your age can afford. (Looking to ANDREE) Well?

ANDREE. (Slamming magazine on table front of sofa) Oh, here it is!

MME. ALVAREZ. *(Crossing, picks up magazine)* Let me see it!

ANDREE. It's the first-act finale of "If I Were King."

MME. ALVAREZ. And where, may I ask, are you?

ANDREE. *(Indicating)* There.

(MME. ALVAREZ *looks at her, and* ANDREE *points to a definite spot.)*

—standing behind that grenadier.

MME. ALVAREZ. Oh! That ear sticking out from the man's neck! One good shove would have put you right into the picture.

ANDREE. *(Taking magazine from her, closing it, and putting it on sofa)* That's the way it always is! Well, goodbye, Maman—don't save any dinner for me. I'll get something at the little cafe near the theater. *(Kisses her cheek.)*

MME. ALVAREZ. You'll do nothing of the kind, dear. There's plenty of time between the matinee and evening for you to run home and have a plate of nice, warm, nourishing cassoulet. *(Returns to Right of GIGI and completes removal of paper-curlers.)*

ANDREE. All right, Maman. *(To GIGI)* Goodbye, monkey! *(Starts toward front door.)*

GIGI. Goodbye, Mama! You promised me you were going to teach me how to crochet—

MME. ALVAREZ. Crochet—uh!

GIGI. When will you do it?

ANDREE. *(Coming back to Left of GIGI)* As soon as I'm up in the new part, darling.

GIGI. *(Putting arm around ANDREE's waist)* I wish it were today!

MME. ALVAREZ. You two are exactly alike. And nobody can budge you.

ANDREE. *(Holdng GIGI's head in her arms)* Well, admit we've got strong characters!

MME. ALVAREZ. Characters! The first thing you know, *you'll* have the child hanging out around a Post and Telegraph Office!

GIGI. Grandma, why would I do that?

MME. ALVAREZ. Because it's the most shiftless thing anyone *can* do!

ANDREE. *(Looking at* GIGI) Never mind, Gigi dear, we're happy, aren't we?

GIGI. *(Her mouth full of licorice)* Uh-hmm!

ANDREE. Um-hmm! What a way to talk! *(Kisses her)* Goodbye, dear— *(Crossing up to alcove)* Have a good day with Aunt Alicia!

GIGI. I'd rather be with you!

ANDREE. Oh well, one can't have everything! *(Exits front door.)*

MME. ALVAREZ. *(As she finishes* GIGI's *curls)* There you are, dear—now, run along!

GIGI. *(Rises, and goes into bedroom)* Shall I wear my everyday coat?—it's good enough.

MME. ALVAREZ. *(Brushing hairs from comb)* And how is one to know it's Sunday, if you do? *(Crosses, gets tray with curling-iron, etc., and takes to sideboard)* Put on your navy blue—and your sailor hat. And don't forget your gloves, Gigi!

    *(*GIGI *returns, wearing coat and hat; crosses to below sofa.* MME. ALVAREZ, *coming down to Right Center.)*

And where are your gloves?

GIGI. *(Standing with her feet apart)* In my pocket.

MME. ALVAREZ. Now let me look you over!—Can't you keep your legs together? When you stand like that, the river Seine could flow between them.

    *(*GIGI *corrects posture.)*

You haven't the single shadow of a stomach, and yet you find some means of sticking it out!

    (Three sharp rings of DOORBELL.)

GIGI. It's Tonton!

    (She rushes into the foyer, to open the door on a young man of 30, whom she grabs and hugs ecstatically.)

Tonton! Tonton! Tonton! ! !

(MME. ALVAREZ *removes apron quickly, crossing above
sofa, and hides it on piano stool, as* TONTON *enters
to up Left Center. He is a tall man, of the greatest
chic, and at the moment appears to be in a mood
of deep dejection.*)

MME. ALVAREZ. *(Goes to him)* Gaston! What a surprise!

GASTON. Mamita!

MME. ALVAREZ. But why aren't you at Nice?

GASTON. *(Putting hat and stick on table)* Oh—something came up.

GIGI. *(Who has crossed Right of table to front of it)*
I know! You've broken it off with Liane!

MME. ALVAREZ. *(Two steps to him)* Why, Gaston—
is that true?

(GASTON *sighs and starts removing his gloves.*)

GIGI. They tell about it in *Gil Blas.*

MME. ALVAREZ. No! ! *(Crosses to sofa, gets copy of
paper.)*

GIGI. One of the girls at school cut it out, and brought
it to me, because she knows that we know you.

GASTON. Really, Gigi!

GIGI. But nobody at school blames you, Tonton. They
all say Liane's behavior hasn't been what it should be—
ever since you first started to keep her.

MME. ALVAREZ. Gilberte! *(Referring to paper)* Ah,
here it is! "Shock For Sugar King."

(GASTON *and* MME. ALVAREZ *exchange glance.*)
"There's a certain bitterness seeping into the beet-sugar
fortune of Gaston Lachaille these days,—and—"

GASTON. Please, Mamita!

MME. ALVAREZ. I'm sorry, Gaston! *(Reads the remainder of the article to herself.)*

GIGI. *(Rushing to look out of the window)* What car
are you using today, Tonton? Ohhh, it's the new Dion-
Bouton landaulette. I've heard that *you* can drive it with
one hand.

GASTON. *(Crossing to Right end of arch)* Oh, anybody can do that!

MME. ALVAREZ. *(Looking to* GASTON*)* Tsk, tsk! Oh, how embarrassing!

    *(*GASTON *returns her look. Quickly to* GIGI, *who is still at window)*

Say goodbye to M. Lachaille, and be off, Gilberte!

GIGI. *(Coming to Left of* GASTON*)* What a shame! I have to go to Aunt Alicia's for my lesson. We could have had such a lovely game of piquet.

GASTON. We'll do it next time.

GIGI. All right. *(Crossing to* MME. ALVAREZ*)* Remember, that's a promise. Goodbye, Grandma. *(Kisses her.)*

MME. ALVAREZ. Goodbye, dear.

GIGI. *(Jumping over chair Left of table, to up Center)* Goodbye, Tonton!

GASTON. Oh, Gigi! Would you like to have the chauffeur take you to Aunt Alicia's in the car?

GIGI. *(Stopping suddenly by foyer)* Tonton!

GASTON. Then you can send it back.

GIGI. *(Rushing Right of table, and throws her arms about* GASTON*)* Oh, Tonton!

MME. ALVAREZ. *(From up Left Center)* You spoil her, Gaston.

GASTON. Oh, it's nothing!

GIGI. Nothing! Nothing— *(Turning to* MME. ALVAREZ*)* to hear the concierge gasp, when I step into that terrific car! *(To* GASTON*)* May I keep it long enough for Aunt Alicia to see?

GASTON. Go ahead!

GIGI. Oh, Tonton!

MME. ALVAREZ. Run along, Gigi!

GIGI. Well, here I go! ! *(Jumps over chair Left of table, and out the front door.)*

MME. ALVAREZ. *(Few steps toward* GASTON*)* Look, Gaston—what exactly happened about—?

GASTON. *(A few steps to her)* Mamita—will you make me a cup of camomile?

MME. ALVAREZ. Of course! We'll have one together. *(Exits into kitchen.)*

(LIGHTS. Start dim sun through window.)

(GASTON gives a deep sigh of depression, reaches for his monocle and inserts it in his eye. After which, we hear a CLOCK strike one. Sounds of dishes and teapot come from the kitchen, as GASTON sits in armchair by fireplace. He rises quickly, to discover he has sat on a ball of yarn and two knitting-needles, which he tosses onto the mantelpiece. He sees GIGI's box of rat-tails (licorice), and says:)

GASTON. Will Gigi mind if I eat one of her rat-tails?

MME. ALVAREZ. *(From kitchen)* How could she? You brought them to her.

GASTON. *(Takes rat-tail and is about to sit on chair below fireplace, when suddenly reminded of needles— making sure the chair is clear, he sits)* Anything new with Aunt Alicia?

MME. ALVAREZ. *(Entering with tray on which are two cups of camomile-tea, spoons, and tea-pot, which she carries and rests on top of stove in fireplace)* No! You know how it is with my sister—she's always the same. Says she prefers to live in her beautiful past than in an ugly present. *(Sitting in armchair)* Alicia and her 'King of Spain,' her 'Duke of Milan,' her 'Khedive,' her 'Rajahs,' in packages of six, if you want to believe her.

GASTON. According to the stories my father told me, she really knew them.

MME. ALVAREZ. Oh, there's no doubt she did. But when we were young, I didn't move in her exalted circle.

GASTON. Just the same, you made romantic history yourself, Mamita.

MME. ALVAREZ. Yes, Gaston— Alicia never boasted anyone more distinguished than my Senor Alvarez. He was the love of my life, Gaston. What a saint! And with a wife who was a devil.

GASTON. *(Stretching his legs out in front of him, in a relaxed position)* Yes? Well, marraige is the one trouble I know how to keep out of.   *(WARN Curtain.)*

MME. ALVAREZ. How right you are, my boy! And yet, when Senor Alvarez passed on, something came over me to take his name. That's when I started calling myself Alvarez—in his memory. *(Adopting a sacred poise, by folding her hands in an attitude of prayer)* And from that very moment, I actually began to *look* Spanish!

GASTON. *(Turning slowly to look at her)* It's extraordinary, Manita—but you really *do!*

MME. ALVAREZ. Of course, my dark hair gave me a good start. Then, it was easy to use white face-powder, lip-rouge, and lots of eye-shadow.

GASTON. And you rounded out the whole effect by taking the given name of Inez.

MME. ALVAREZ. *(Looking at clock on mantel)* Ah, two minutes!—it's ready! *(Hands GASTON his cup of tea)* If I'm not indiscreet, Gaston—how *did* your break with Liane come about?

GASTON. Let's not go into it now, Mamita! I've had to listen to jokes about it all day long. The sad thing is that most of them are pretty funny.

MME. ALVAREZ. My poor boy! You weren't even twenty, when I intervened for you in that quarrel with Maryse Chuquet.

GASTON. Was that Maryse,—or was it?

MME. ALVAREZ. Yes,—it was Maryse—the trollop! I knew she'd leave you again, but since she was in your blood, I did the best I could to get your mistress back for you—as if you were my own son!

GASTON. Dear Mamita! You've been better than a mother to me, always. That's why I came here today—the one place in all Paris, where I can relax, and forget that, with all my money, I had to catch Liane in bed with someone else. *(Dropping his head in complete dejection.)*

MME. ALVAREZ. *(Hastening to console him, rises, to*

him) My poor Gaston! Have a little more camomile—
it will help you to forget!

(LIGHTS fade.)

THE CURTAIN FALLS

ACT ONE

Scene II

SCENE: *A tiny set which reveals a corner of the boudoir
on the second floor of the small but exquisite house
of Gigi's Aunt Alicia. It is very costly and like a
jewel case. As a criticism, one might say it is a little
bit TOO MUCH like a jewel case—that it lacks
warmth and is anything but homelike. The whole
atmosphere is one of discreet luxury. The carpet,
covered by Aubusson rugs, gives wings to one's feet.*

*The woodwork is gilt. There is a door Right, lead-
ing to downstairs, and one at Left leading to the
bedrooms. At Center is a large window, looking out
onto the streets of Paris. Niches Right and Left of
window are filled with bits and pieces—evidently
ALICIA'S knick-knacks of the past. The green walls
are panelled in baroque gold, and in each panel is a
delicate painting.*

*Right and Left, in down stage corners, are gold
fixture-stands, holding assorted evergreens.*

*A straight gold chair at Right. A gold lace-uphol-
stered chaise-longue at Left, above which is a small
table with telephone, note-pad, etc. At Left end of
chaise-lounge is a low, gilt stand—a gold foot-stool
near Right end of chaise-lounge. A floor-lamp (gilt)
it at Right of window. A bell-pull hangs on up stage
side of door Left, a desk down Left.*

AT RISE: ALICIA'S *butler,* VICTOR, *is ushering in* GIGI,
and at the same time bearing a glass of water and

*a small pill-box on a silver tray. He goes to down
Left of chaise-longue.*

GIGI. *(Enters to Right of window)* I'll bet you were
surprised, when I pointed out my car down there, weren't
you, Victor?

VICTOR. Surprised is putting it very mildly, Mademoiselle.

GIGI. And what did you think—I mean at first?

VICTOR. I said to myself, there's only one thing left
for Mademoiselle Gilberte now, and that is—

GIGI. What?

VICTOR. To arrive in a balloon!

GIGI. Really? Let's take another look at it from here!

*(She runs to the window, looks out, and whistles to
the chauffeur below. French motor HORN responds
to* GIGI'S *whistle, as* VICTOR *puts the tray on small
stand Left. She is interrupted by the entrance Left
of* AUNT ALICIA. *She is seventy years old—dainty
as porcelain, but with a robust health, which she
hides under affectations of frailty. She is wearing an
exquisite dressing-gown of pink chiffon, and her head
is partially covered with a cream lace fichu—she
enters to Left of window.)*

ALICIA. Gilberte!

GIGI. *(Turning quickly to her)* Oh! Good afternoon,
Aunty!

(Few steps to ALICIA, *leans her forehead forward,
which* ALICIA *kisses.)*

You've got your headache again, Aunt Alicia, haven't
you?

ALICIA. Yes, Gilberte.

(VICTOR picks up tray.)

GIGI. I always know you've got it, when you wear that
lace thing on your hair.

ALICIA. That lace thing, Gilberte, is called a fichu. *(Starts down Center to edge of chaise-lounge)* This one happened to belong to a Queen of France.

*(*GIGI *gives a low whistle as* VICTOR *serves* ALICIA *the pill and glass of water.* ALICIA *gives* GIGI *a disapproving look, and* VICTOR *attempts to warn* GIGI *with a quick glance.* ALICIA *catches this, but proceeds to take pill and water.)*

VICTOR. Is that all, Madame?
ALICIA. Thank you, Victor.

(This is his dismissal and VICTOR *exits Left.)*

GIGI. Since you've got your headache, Aunty, perhaps I won't have to—I mean, perhaps you don't *want* to give me my lesson today—
ALICIA. That's right, dear. You may stop in the kitchen on your way out, and pick up a cake you're to take along.
GIGI. Oh, thanks, Aunt Alicia. What kind is it today?
ALICIA. Mocha, I believe.
GIGI. Oh! *(Rushes to door Right.)*
ALICIA. You'd better sit down and rest for five minutes before you start.
GIGI. *(In doorway)* Oh, I'm not the least bit tired. *(Assuming a very casual pose)* I came over in a car.
ALICIA. In a car?
GIGI. *(With her usual excitement)* In Tonton's Dion-Bouton landaulette! He's at the house with Grandma now. *(Rushes to window, and says)* Look!
ALICIA. *(Following her to Left of window)* Gaston Lachaille in town?! But this is the week of the Flower Fete in Nice!
GIGI. He didn't go this time, because he's broken with Liane. *(Leans out window, and calls)* Oh, Al-bert!

(She is answered by a HORN.)

ALICIA. He's *what?*

GIGI. *(Turning to* ALICIA*)* He's broken it off with Liane! *(Leans out window again, and calls)* Oh, Albert! Don't go away! I'm riding back with you!

(She is answered by TWO HORNS.)

ALICIA. *(Pulling* GIGI *away from window)* Gilberte— one doesn't give orders to a servant from a second-floor window, my dear!

GIGI. I'm sorry, Aunt Alicia. Oh, Aunty, you should have seen me driving over here. I pretended to be bored, like this— *(Gives her impression of an elegant lady, bouncing with the motion of a car)* But I could see people were looking, out of the corner of my eye. And at the Eiffel Tower, a very elegant man tipped his hat— *(Gesture of hat-tipping)* —to *me*. It was just as I had suddenly grown up to be a fashionable young lady.

ALICIA. *(Looking her over, deeply thoughtful)* It was, eh?

GIGI. *(Holding her head forward for a quick kiss)* Goodbye, Aunty. Please watch me from the window when I drive off, will you? *(Dashes for door.)*

ALICIA. Gilberte! Wait a minute—don't be in such a hurry!

GIGI. But I—

ALICIA. Sit down a moment.

*(*GIGI *hesitates.)*

Sit down!

*(*GIGI *sits chair Right, reluctantly.* ALICIA *crosses down to her.)*

So, M. Lachaille and Mlle. Liane have come to the parting of the ways, eh?

GIGI. Yes.

ALICIA. You seem to be sad about it.

GIGI. Of course I am. *(Childishly lifts foot to the opposite knee, and toys with shoe)* It's going to take all Tonton's time, to pick out someone new. He won't come to the house any more to play piquet, or drink camomile, or bring me licorice. It'll be pretty gloomy for me.

ALICIA. Do you know anything about this break-up?

GIGI. *(Turns on chair, facing* ALICIA*)* Well— *(Suddenly realizing what she is about to answer)* But I'm not supposed to repeat gossip, am I?

ALICIA. This time you may tell me what you have heard, Gilberte.

GIGI. *(Pulling chair a bit closer to* ALICIA, *and assuming the attitude of a little gossip)* Well—you see—one of the girls at school—Lydia Poret—has a mother who goes skating all the time at the Palais de Glace. So she heard all about it there. She says Liane waited around for her birthday present, and then skipped off—

ALICIA. One doesn't say skipped off, Gilberte, even of a person whose behavior is completely uncivilized. *(Then, forgetting herself)* But where did she skip off—I mean, where did she disappear to?

GIGI. *(Pulling her chair a bit closer)* Well, she made the mistake of trying to hide some place in Normandy that's pretty small. So it wasn't very hard for Tonton to find out that there were only two bedrooms at the Inn, and that Liane was in one of them, and a skating professor from the Palais de Glace, named Sandomar, was in the other.

ALICIA. Sandomar! *(Intrigued)* He's the one who skates with Polaire every day at five o'clock. *(More to herself)* What a physique that man has got!

GIGI. *(Not very interested)* Has he?

ALICIA. Never mind! *(Few steps up Left Center)* Do you know what sort of a birthday gift Lachaille gave her?

GIGI. Why yes—it was a string of thirty-seven monstrous pearls. The one in the middle is as big as Mme. Poret's thumb. *(Attempts to indicate its size, with her thumb. Then finds it requires both thumbs.)*

ALICIA. Hmmm! Rich as he is, I'd hardly have thought Lachaille was *that* generous.

GIGI. *(Relaxing against the back of her chair)* Oh, Mme. Poret said Tonton tried at first to give Liane a string of small ones. But she absolutely demanded those monsters.

ALICIA. She knows how to conduct herself when she wants to, that young lady.

GIGI. *(Rises, crossing to* ALICIA*)* Goodbye, Aunty—until next week.

ALICIA. *(Patting* GIGI's *cheek)* Goodbye, Gilberte. You'll go straight home, dear, won't you?

GIGI. Will I? Of course I will. Why now, I can have a game of piquet with Tonton.

ALICIA. Tonton! Will Tonton still be there?

GIGI. Of course! He can't leave without his car, Aunty. Anyway, he's always good for at least two cups of camomile with Grandma.

ALICIA. Take off your coat! *(As* GIGI *reluctantly complies, looks her over with distaste)* Ravishing! Turn around!

*(*GIGI *obeys.)*

Where did you ever get that garment?

GIGI. It's an old dress of Mama's that Grandma made over for me.

ALICIA. It looks it. You·shouldn't even play piquet in that, with your grandmother.

GIGI. Oh, but Tonton's seen me in this dozens of times. *(Slips the coat on one arm)* I'll be back next Sunday, Aunt Alicia.

ALICIA. Just a moment! I think it's very wrong of me to neglect your lessons—even though I have a headache.

GIGI. Oh, Aunt Alicia!

ALICIA. You're so rapidly getting to be a young lady, my dear, that one doesn't dare waste a moment.

GIGI. Oh, but Aunty—

ALICIA. Take off your hat, Gilberte! *(*ALICIA *crosses above chaise-longue, and pulls bell-rope)* You will remain here for your lunch, and your lesson.

GIGI. *(With all her patience, complies)* All right, Aunty. But I'll have to send Tonton's car back. *(Starts to window, to call.)*

ALICIA. *(A few steps toward her)* Come away from that window, child! Victor will dismiss the car properly for you. *(Starts for door Left)* Sit down while I fetch something for your lession. It's going to be important today—very important. *(Exits Left.)*

(GIGI, *left alone, gives vent to her disappointment, and temper, pulls hat from her head and throws it violently to the floor, then does likewise with her coat. After which she kicks the Right end of the chaise-longue.)*

VICTOR. (VICTOR *enters Right in time to catch this display of childish temper)* You're right, Mademoiselle— I never liked that thing myself!

GIGI. *(Now hopping about on one foot, holding the other, recently injured)* Don't joke, Victor! I want—I mean, *she* wants you to send M. Lachaille's car back.

(Enter ALICIA, with jewel-box and keys.)

VICTOR. Very well, Mademoiselle.

ALICIA. *(Putting jewel-box on small stand Left)* Oh, Victor!

VICTOR. Yes, Madame?

ALICIA. You may serve luncheon today for two, but give us a half hour for Mlle. Gilberte to have her lesson first.

VICTOR. Very well, Madame. *(Picks up GIGI's hat and coat from floor, and exits Right.)*

ALICIA. *(Sitting Left end of chaise-longue)* Gilberte— just how old are you, exactly?

GIGI. *(Who is still up Center)* Same as the other day, Aunty—sixteen.

ALICIA. Whom do you have as friends?

GIGI. *(Limping to front of chaise-longue)* Nobody. Grandma only allows me to play with the very little children. She doesn't want me going around with anyone my own age.

ALICIA. She's right, for once.

GIGI. Oh, but I do adore the little ones. It's such fun to play house, and pretend that I'm their mother.

ALICIA. And that amuses you?

GIGI. Oh yes—they're so divine, those youngsters! *(Sits Right end of chaise-longue)* I wish they belonged to me, every one of them.

ALICIA. Perhaps it's just as well they don't. *(Taking GIGI's hands in hers)* Now, tell me, Gilberte, whether or not you've got any bees in your bonnet?

GIGI. Bees in my bonnet?

ALICIA. Any young men hanging about? Any college student with his books still under his arm? Any middle-aged gentleman? If you lie, I'll know it.

GIGI. But there's nobody, Aunty. Has someone been telling stories about me?

ALICIA. *(Patting her cheek)* No, child. I just wanted to be sure. *(Gets jewel-box keys.)*

GIGI. But why does Grandma forbid me to accept any invitations?

ALICIA. Because you'd only be asked out by ordinary people, who wouldn't be of any use to you.

GIGI. And we're not ordinary people?

ALICIA. No, indeed, we are not!

GIGI. But what makes us different from those ordinary people, Aunty?

ALICIA. In the main, Gilberte, it's because they marry.

GIGI. Is that the reason why I'm forbidden ever to talk to any young men?

ALICIA. Yes. *(Turns and unlocks jewel-box)*

GIGI. But, Aunty, why is it we're not supposed to get married?

ALICIA. *(Turning to her)* Well, marraige with us is not forbidden. But in place of marrying at first, it's always possble that we may marry at last.

GIGI. But why not at first?

ALICIA. Because if we marry at first, he's certain to be the sort who will—vulgarize us.

GIGI. You mean somebody like a shopkeeper?

ALICIA. Exactly.

GIGI. But won't he be just the same sort, if we marry him at last?

ALICIA. Yes—he's likely to be. But by that time, one has one's memories. *(Lifts stand with jewel-box to between GIGI and herself, and opens box, displaying array of jewels)* Now, we'll begin the lesson for today.

GIGI. *(Slides to sit on footstool, front of chaise-longue)* Oh— Oh, Auuty!

ALICIA. You never dreamed I had so many jewels, did you?

GIGI. I didn't know there were that many in all of France!

ALICIA. *(Takes ring from box, and holds it up for inspection)* Now—what is this, Gilberte?

GIGI. *(Being the attentive pupil)* A diamond.

ALICIA. What kind?

GIGI. A—an oblong one.

ALICIA. Yes. *(Putting ring on GIGI's finger)* And the weight of it is five carats.

GIGI. It is?

ALICIA. *(Taking another jewel)* Now, take these diamonds, which are set around this ruby. Their weight is half a carat each. *(Pins jewel on GIGI's dress)* Anything less than that, I call a chip. Will you remember that?

GIGI. Yes, Aunty.

ALICIA. *(Selecting another jewel)* Ah, this ring! What memories it brings up!

GIGI. It's a very large stone, Aunty.

ALICIA. It was given to me by my mother, when I was only fifteen. She put it on my finger and said always wear this, my child, and nobody will ever dare give you one that's smaller—and it worked. *(Puts ring on GIGI. Picking up another jewel)* Now—what is this?

GIGI. *(Studies it)* Mmmmmm—a—topaz?

ALICIA. A topaz?—A topaz, among my jewels!

GIGI. I'm sorry, Aunty.

ALICIA. Why not an agate? Or a cat's eye.

GIGI. Then—then what *is* it, Aunt Alicia?

ALICIA. It's a jonquil diamond, you little barbarian. *(Holding ring closer to GIGI)* And study it closely for color—or you'll wind up your career *with* topazes. *(Puts ring on* GIGI, *and reaches for another ring)* And—this?

GIGI. *(Entranced)* Why, that's an emerald!

(ALICIA *puts ring on her.)*

Ohh—it's beautiful!

ALICIA. There are very few emeralds in this world that have ever possessed such a miracle of evanescent blue.

GIGI. Who gave you that emerald, Aunty?

ALICIA. A king.

GIGI. *(Holding the rings at arm's length, surveying them)* A great king?

ALICIA. No,—a little one. Great kings don't give away very valuable stones.

GIGI. Why not?

ALICIA. If you want my opinion, it's because they're rather stingy. But you must learn never to accept a second-rate jewel, even from a king.

GIGI. *(Reverently)* Yes, Aunt Alicia.

ALICIA. It's much better to wait until first-rate ones come along.

GIGI. What if they don't come along?

ALICIA. *(Removing the jewels from* GIGI's *hands, and returning them to box)* Then hold firmly to your ideals just the same. Better wear a ring that cost 100 sous, than a bad diamond costing 3000 francs. At least you can say it's a memento from some female relative.

GIGI. Aunty, *who* does give away the most valuable jewels?

ALICIA. Men who are timid—men who are conceited. Climbers, because they think giving away monstrous jewels is proof of culture. And, speaking of culture, never under any circumstances, wear artistic jewels, And *always* protect yourself against family heirlooms. *(Moves stand with jewel-box to its original position.)*

GIGI. But Grandma wears a very beautiful cameo around her neck, on a ribbon.

ALICIA. There is no such thing as a beautiful cameo! You must only recognize precious stones and pearls.

GIGI. *(Stretching her legs forward, and leaning back against the chaise-longue)* Aunty, I just adore opals!

ALICIA. That's all right, dear,—so long as you don't wear them.

GIGI. You think they bring people bad luck?

ALICIA. I think nothing of the kind. But a good, healthy set of superstitions is a necessity when dealing with men.

GIGI. Why, Aunty?

ALICIA. Because the poor things are not as intelligent as we are. So it's only good manners to play the fool for them. That's where superstitions come in handy.

GIGI. *(Trying to show real interest in things)* Aunty— what is a bracelet set in—malachite?

ALICIA. Always a calamity! Where did you ever hear of such a thing?*(Rising)* Get.up, child! Stand over there!

> (GIGI *rises, and moves as indicated to Right Center.* ALICIA *follows to just Left of her, lifting* GIGI'S *head to the light.)*

Beautiful jaws, my child! *(Using her hands to open* GIGI'S *mouth)* What teeth! *(A step back from her)* What teeth, I'd have been able to eat up all of France.

> (GIGI *closes her mouth.)*

As it was, I was able to get away with rather a large slice of it. *(Resuming her inspection of* GIGI) An impossible little nose—undistinguished mouth—cheekbones like a Russian moujik's—

GIGI. *(Distressed)* Oh, Aunty!

ALICIA. *(Taking a step up to observe her in profile)* Never mind—you have all the equipment necessary in your eyes, your eyelashes, your teeth, and your hair— and as for your figure—possibilities— *(She makes a gesture with the back of her hand toward* GIGI, *and slowly outlines the contour of her bosom)* Very nice—possibilities.

> (GIGI'S *eyes drop to observe first the right and then left breast.)*

I wonder if you're going to have any taste in dress. When you think of being well turned out, Gilberte, how do you see yourself?

GIGI. *(With great excitement)* Oh, but I understand

very well what's becoming to me, Aunty! I saw the picture of a dress in a fashion-book, that was designed for Mme. Lucie Gerard. Hundreds of little pin-tucks in pearl-grey chiffon, from top to bottom— *(Gestures elaborately, to describe the effect.)*

ALICIA. Don't gesticulate, dear. It makes you look common.

GIGI. And I saw another picture—in color—a dress of brocade, a sort of lavender blue, on a background of black velvet—cut—cut, so that the train looks like the tail of a peacock! *(Another gesture describing the tail of the peacock.)*

ALICIA. Just like an actress!

GIGI. *(Pleased with herself)* Yes.

ALICIA. It wasn't meant as a compliment. I tell you what I'm going to do, child— *(Takes note-pad and pencil from table back of chaise-longue, and crossing front of chaise-longue, sits Left end of it)* I'm going to give you a note to the head saleswoman at Paquin.

GIGI. *(Excited)* Pa—Pa—

ALICIA. *(Starts to scratch off note)* Paquin. She's an old colleague of mine—she failed and had to go to work.

GIGI. Oh, Aunt Alicia—a dress from Paquin's!! *(Crosses to Right end of chaise-longue.)*

ALICIA. But I thought you weren't interested in clothes?

GIGI. I'm just not interested in the clothes they make me at the house.

ALICIA. *(Folding the note)* I don't wonder! Here, child. One who risks nothing, gains nothing.

GIGI. *(Kneeling on chaise-longue, arms around ALICIA)* Oh, Aunty—thanks, thanks, thanks!

ALICIA. Not too rough, dear. Don't disarrange my hair! *(Knock on the door Right.)* Come in.

VICTOR. *(Enters)* Luncheon is served, Madame.

ALICIA. *(Rising, takes jewel-box, starts for bedroom door)* We'll be down directly. *(Exits Left.)*

(VICTOR *replaces chair Right, as* GIGI *goes to Left of him.*)

GIGI. *(Half whispers it)* Hoy, Victor! What do I have to learn how to eat today?

VICTOR. For the first course, there will be eggs, brouilles, mousseline a l'Imperatrice.

GIGI. Are they going to be very complicated?

VICTOR. Merely scrambled. The entree will be ortolans.

GIGI. Oh, those nasty little birds!   *(WARN Curtain.)*

VICTOR. But the ortolans need not be complicated, either, if you cut them in two— *(Using his finger to indicate knife)* with one stroke of your knife. Do it with authority, and then pop the entire half in your mouth.

GIGI. Bones and all?

VICTOR. Bones and all!

GIGI. Oh, dear!

VICTOR. But the bones of an ortolan really make little, if any, difference, Madamoiselle.

GIGI. Maybe not, but you know my Aunt! She'll go right on asking questions that I'll have to answer with my whole mouth full of bird bones.

ALICIA. *(Enters)* I thought I told you, Victor, that we would be down presently.

VICTOR. Yes, Madame. *(Exits Right.)*

ALICIA. *(To above chaise-longue)* Now, my dear, if you'd like to help a poor, feeble old lady down to the dining-room.

(GIGI, *crossing to above* ALICIA, *offers her arm, and they both start to Center.*)

When luncheon is over, remind me to teach you how to choose a cigar.

GIGI. *(Stopping suddenly, and swinging to front of* ALICIA) Aunty! I don't have to smoke a cigar!

ALICIA. Certainly not. But a woman who learns a man's preference in everything is always well armed against him.

(GIGI *starts toward door Right.*)

Take care—don't walk like a grenadier! Put one foot in front of the other—
> (GIGI *obeys, but in looking back at* ALICIA, *is about to bump into the chair Right.*)

Look where you're going!
> (GIGI *comes to a sudden stop and pivots, to head for door.*)

Not so stiff! Hold your head up! A woman should float, like a swan.
> (GIGI *stiffly raises her arms to waist-high position, thereby giving the effect of a bird in full wing, and proceeds through door.* ALICIA *follows.*)

Put your arms down, child—hold your head up—walk gracefully—that's better—

(LIGHTS fade, and the Curtain falls.)

ACT ONE

SCENE III

One hour later. Mme. Alvarez's living room.

GASTON *is still with* MME. ALVAREZ. *They have long since finished their camomile, and* GASTON, *with the floodgates of his reserve finally opened, is pacing from Right to Left, going into the agonizing details of his plight with his mistress.* MME. ALVAREZ *is seated on sofa, Left, with basket of darning. She darns as she listens.*

GASTON. So that's the whole story, Mamita. *(Sits on sofa, Center)* But I keep on asking myself: What is it they require, these women, in order to be faithful?

MME. ALVAREZ. Yes, who can one trust these days, Gaston? It's very baffling.

GASTON. I've always tried to be generous with misstresses, I think. But the conniving that goes on—and even worse. Sometimes I feel as if I'm living with some thief for a roommate. Sometimes I even hide my diamond cuff-links. *(Taking from his pocket a gold cigarette case, studded with jewels)* And this cigarette case!

MME. ALVAREZ. Poor Gaston!

GASTON. You may believe it or not, Mamita, but sometimes in a hotel bedroom I've even thought of trying to find a place to hide my sable-lined overcoat.

MME. ALVAREZ. And yet people think the rich don't have their troubles!

GASTON. Troubles! Hah! Why, the only money I ever spend without feeling I'm being cheated, is when I make a donation to some charity, because I realize in advance that I needn't expect any return.

MME. ALVAREZ. Like throwing it out of the window, eh?

GASTON. That's right. But don't think I'm over extravagant, Mamita!

MME. ALVAREZ. Oh, I don't!

GASTON. Why, even when I bought my yacht, I first made sure that the King of Bulgaria was after it. So three months later, I sold it to him at a very nice profit. Same thing when I purchased that newspaper. Yes, I can always *make* money, but the problem is, how to *hang on* to it. There isn't a single moment when I don't have to be on my guard.

MME. ALVAREZ. But what a dreadful way of living, Gaston!

GASTON. Isn't it? *(Looking three-quarters front)* I never look into my mirror in the morning, without saying to myself: somewhere in Paris there's some other man who's enjoying the favors that *I'm* paying for in good, hard cash!

MME. ALVAREZ. And to think he's only a skating teacher.

GASTON. Yes—I simply can't understand it, when I'm such an excellent skater myself!

MME. ALVAREZ. I'm afraid Liane is basically pretty vulgar!

GASTON. Yes. Well—ha, ha, ha! *(Rises, and crosses toward mantel)* —I'll economize on a decorated carriage for the Flower Fete, anyway! *(Glances at clock)* I say, look at the time, will you?! And I've an important engagement at the Jockey Club!

MME. ALVAREZ. *(Rises, to front of dining table)* That's right, my dear. Try to see as much of your young friends as possible.

GASTON. *(Crossing to her)* That's just what I intend to do. Thank you, Mamita— *(Shakes hands with her)* And thanks for the camomile.

GIGI. *(Enters front door, out of breath)* Ouff! When I saw Tonton's car was still outside, I fairly flew upstairs! *(To above table)* Now, Tonton—have you got time for our game of piquet?

GASTON. *(Who has backed a few steps to Right when GIGI entered)* Well—some of the fellows are waiting for me at the club—

GIGI. It'll be the same a hundred years from now!

MME. ALVAREZ. You mustn't beg him, Gigi.

GIGI. Come *on*, Tonton!

GASTON. Well, maybe—just one rubber!

GIGI. *(In her excitement, jumps over chair Right of table, to emptied box of licorice)* I'll get the cards!!

(GASTON *pulls out chair Right of table for* GIGI. *She crosses to it, and sits at table, preparing for card game.* GASTON *crosses above table, and sits Left of it.)*

MME. ALVAREZ. And how did you find your Aunt Alicia?

GIGI. Well, at first she said she had her headache—

MME. ALVAREZ. *(Crossing to chair down Right, with her mending, sits)* As if she ever had a headache in her whole, entire life!

GIGI. *(Preparing cards for cutting)* Then she changed her mind, and decided I was growing up, and ought to learn all about carats—not the vegetable, you know, but the measure of a diamond.

GASTON. Good heavens, young woman!

GIGI. *(Discovering the empty licorice box)* Who's eaten up all my licorice? *(Gives a quick look to* MME. ALVAREZ, *then to* GASTON) Tonton! Now, was that nice?

GASTON. Say! Did I eat *all* of them?

GIGI. Yes, and you've got to bring me another box.

GASTON. I'll send you one. I'm off to Switzerland to-morrow.

GIGI. Well, see that you don't forget it. *(Turning on her chair, faces* MME. ALVAREZ) Oh, there's the most tremendous news, Grandma. I'm to have a dress from Paquin—

GASTON. Paquin?

GIGI. One to play cards in with Tonton— Aunty said so!

MME. ALVAREZ. *(Thoughtfully)* Really?

GIGI. That'll be chic, won't it?

GASTON. It most certainly will.

GIGI. *(Leaning on table, her legs still draped alongside of her chair)* All ready, partner?

MME. ALVAREZ. Gigi dear—pull down your skirt!

(GIGI obeys, and corrects her position.)

GASTON. I'll play you for ten pounds of sugar.
                              (LIGHTS start exterior dim.)

GIGI. Oh—*that* stuff!

MME. ALVAREZ. Gigi, where is your respect?

GIGI. Well, Tonton always wants to bet with sugar, because he gets it for nothing!

MME. ALVAREZ. Gilberte!

GASTON. Let her alone, Mamita! What do you want to play for, then?

GIGI. Any suggestions?

GASTON. Some silk stockings?

GIGI. No. Silk stockings itch my legs. *(Shoves pack of cards towards* GASTON) Cut, Tonton! *(She leans on table, and strikes a contemplative mood, while winding a strand of hair about the end of her nose)* Let—me—see—I think I'd rather have a—

MME. ALVAREZ. Gigi,—that's not a very elegant gesture, my dear.

GIGI. Oh. *(Turns to table, cuts cards, and says)* Well, my deal! *(Starts to deal cards) I* know what I'd like to win—but it's expensive.

GASTON. *(Picking up his cards)* All right—out with it!

GIGI. *(Still dealing)* A Nile-green corset, with garters embroidered in moss roses.

(GASTON *whistles.*)

MME. ALVAREZ. Now really, dear!

GIGI. *(Getting an even better Idea) No!* What I'd like to have most of all, is a music-roll!

GASTON. But you don't take your music to school, do you?

GIGI. *(Picking up her cards, and arranging them)* No —but at school the girls put their lessons in a music-roll, because it makes them look like students at the Conservatory.

MME. ALVAREZ. Gilberte, that's enough nonsense, now.

GASTON. Look out, my friend, I don't need a single card.

GIGI. Don't let that fool you, my partner—I couldn't have picked mine better, if I'd stole them!

ANDREE. (ANDREE *enters Center, carrying the evening paper, "Figaro")* Well— Heavens above—if it isn't Gaston!

(Goes to above table. GASTON *rises, shakes hands with her, during which time* GIGI *grabs his other hand, in which he has his cards, and steals a quick glance at them.)*

GASTON. Oh, Good afternoon, Andree.
ANDREE. Please sit down!

(He does so, and ANDREE *crosses and puts paper on piano, then crosses up to hat-rack, and removes hat.)*

GIGI. What's so unusual about Tonton being here, Maman?

ANDREE. Nothing. But it's a coincidence— *(To above table)* —because everybody was talking about Gaston backstage today. You and your break with Liane.

(MME. ALVAREZ *fakes a distracting cough.*)
Have you a cold, Maman?

GASTON. I wish they'd leave the whole subject alone!

MME. ALVAREZ. But what a compliment, Gaston! The Opera Comique isn't generally up on the gossip of the *past* century!

GIGI. Your play, idiot!

GASTON. Oh, beg your pardon, half-wit!

ANDREE. *(Crossing Right of* GIGI'S *chair, to mantel, fixes hair)* If I could only have telephoned you, Maman, I wouldn't have come home today to dinner.

MME. ALVAREZ. And why not?

ANDREE. I had an invitation to dine out.

MME. ALVAREZ. With someone new? Who is he?

ANDREE. Mademe Le Clerc.

MME. ALVAREZ. Oh!

ANDREE. It was a wonderful chance to go to work on her, and get her to work on her husband, about that part in the new production. *(Crossing up Right of* GIGI'S *chair, looking at* GIGI'S *cards)* Don't you think we ought to have a telephone?

GASTON. Sure! Why don't you, Mamita?

MME. ALVAREZ. Because Andree would be forever talking to some no-account.

ANDREE. *(Has crossed to behind* GASTON, *and looked at his cards)* Maman says we've got to wait until Gigi's grown up enough to have admirers.

(GIGI *has just trumped a play of* GASTON.)

GASTON. Does she? Just a moment, my friend, you're cheating!

GIGI. Liar!

ANDREE. Maman says that telephones are only useful to women when they want to lie to men.

*(She signals to GIGI which card to play. GIGI takes her
cue and plays another card.)*

MME. ALVAREZ. Did you sing well at the matinee, *dear?*

ANDREE. *(Approves of GIGI's strategy)* Yes, very well,
Maman—as usual. *(Crosses down, sits sofa, and starts
reading paper.)*

GASTON. You little robber—you've got that fourth
King up your sleeve!

GIGI. I have not—you big, stupid parrot-nose! *(Kicks
him playfully under the table.)*

MME. ALVAREZ. Children! Children!

ANDREE. Well—here's a picture of Liane in *Figaro!*

MME. ALVAREZ. *(Ready to murder her)* And why not?
The most important liaison in Paris shattered?!

ANDREE. *(Holding paper toward GASTON)* Want to
see it, Gaston?

GIGI. Really, Maman—Tonton knows what she looks
like!

ANDREE. Gaston, if I were you, I'd pay Liane back by
taking someone tremendously important—not just the
first little girl you see, but some woman of the very top
aristocracy!

GASTON. Yes, that might be an idea. *(Turns his attention to card game.)*

MME. ALVAREZ. Andree—you'd have him changing a
one-eyed horse for a blind one!

ANDREE. *(Still busy with her paper)* Somebody around
the theater says there's an acrobat at the Olympia who
has the best chance with you

GASTON. Oh! That one!

MME. ALVAREZ. *(With alarm)* What one?

GASTON. She calls herself "the Cobra."

GIGI. *(Impatiently)* It's your play, stupid!

GASTON. *(Playing card)* I'm sorry, spider-legs!

ANDREE. The Cobra's very pretty, isn't she, Gaston?

GASTON. Ravishing!

MME. ALVAREZ. Really, Andree!—Gaston Lachaille
is not for any mere music-hall entertainer. Give him

credit for supplanting Liane with something completely original!

ANDREE. *(Putting down the paper)* Original! Why, they bring this girl onstage in a basket, no bigger than that— *(Indicates size)* —and she comes out of it, unwinding like a snake *(Demonstrating)* And if that isn't original, what is? *(Rises, crossing to Center)* The entire Jockey Club is absolutely mad about her! *(Her voice reaching a pitch of excitement.)*

MME. ALVAREZ. *(Rising)* Andree, your voice is getting husky! *(Quickly takes teapot from tray on stove, and going to* ANDREE) Go and gargle!

ANDREE. *(Dropping her voice to a whisper)* Oh dear, I hadn't noticed!

MME. ALVAREZ. Here! Take a mouthful of this, and leave it there—leave it an hour! *(She jams teapot in* ANDREE's *abdomen.)*

ANDREE. *(Completely mystified, but anxious to protect her voice)* All right, Maman. *(Takes pot, starts for bedroom; still bewildered, she turns and looks at* MME. ALVAREZ.)

MME. ALVAREZ. Jackass!

*(*ANDREE *exits into bedroom.* MME. ALVAREZ *returns to down Right.)*

GASTON. *(About to make a brilliant play)* So—I'm a stupid parrot-nose, am I? *(Plays his card.)*

GIGI. That's what I said! *(Triumphantly trumps his play.)*

GASTON. You lanky, overgrown weed—you've been cheating again!

GIGI. *(With playful menace, as she slowly begins to rise)* What—did—you—call—me?

(She takes end of large table-cover, throws it over GASTON's *head, and quickly pulls him from his chair, to the floor—they tussle.)*

GASTON. Look out, you're tipping over the table!

GIGI. *(On her knees by his side, pummeling him)* What did you call me? Say it again. Go on.

GASTON. *(Laughingly, as he tries to protect himself)* Gigi, how unladylike!

GIGI. Who wants to be a lady?

MME. ALVAREZ. *(Rising, toes toward them, joyfully)* Stop, Gigi! Please, Gaston, you ought not to encourage her! *(Picks up dining chair knocked over by GASTON.)*

GASTON. Encourage her! Why, she frightens me to death! She's like a wildcat! Look how late she's made me for my appointment!

GIGI. *(Still kneeling over him)* What about my music-roll, Tonton? You know I won it!

GASTON. *(Laughing)* You're getting to be mercenary —just like all the women!

GIGI. But do I get my music-roll? And my licorice?

GASTON. All right. I'll see that you get your music-roll —*and* your licorice!

GIGI. *(Squirming around to Right of him, rests in kneeling position)* That's better!

> *(GASTON gets to his knees, arranging his dishevelled clothes.)*

Where are you going to eat dinner tonight, Tonton?

GASTON. Oh, Maxim's, I suppose,—as usual.

(MME. ALVAREZ is busy straightening things up, near the buffet.)

GIGI. Maxim's? What are you going to eat?

GASTON. Oh—filet of sole, I suppose. And, naturally, breast of pheasant under glass.

GIGI. *Mmmmmmh!* We're going to have warmed-over cassoulet tonight.

MME. ALVAREZ. *(From above table)* It's only a cassoulet with pork. Goose was out of the question this week.

GASTON. *(Getting to his feet. At up Left Center)* I'm going to have them send you a goose from Bon Abri.

MME. ALVAREZ. Oh, thanks—thanks very much, Gaston!

GASTON. *(His mouth watering)* Not that it isn't delicious, too—with pork. *(Tosses off kiss.)*

MME. ALVAREZ. I suppose you couldn't stay and have some?

GASTON. Well—I really oughtn't—

MME. ALVAREZ. It improves, you know—with warming over.

GASTON. Well—no, thanks! *(Crosses foot on arm of sofa, to adjust garter.)*

GIGI. (GIGI *rises quickly, sits on sofa facing upstage, to* GASTON) Oh, please, Tonton—you've *never* had dinner with us!

GASTON. No, I'm sorry, Gigi—not this evening! *(Crossing to above dining-table)* Well, goodbye, Mamita.

MME. ALVAREZ. Goodbye, Gaston.

GASTON. *(To* GIGI) Goodbye, Gigi!

GIGI. *(Jumps up, goes to* GASTON, *up Center, brings him back to archway)* Just a moment, Tonton! Your hair got rumpled in our fight. Here! *(She tries to smooth his hair into place, then wets both palms with her tongue, and plasters the hair into place)* That's better! And now your necktie. *(Lifts his chin, and arranges tie)* There!

(For a moment, she stares at the tie, while GASTON *quietly looks at her. Slowly, their eyes meet, and for a moment there is a silence. We hear the CLOCK strike five. MME. ALVAREZ slowly turns her head and watches them.)*

GASTON. *(Revealing a sudden trace of shyness, gives a selfconcious little laugh and says)* Why,—uh--thanks! *(He steps back and bumps into chair Left of table.)*

GIGI. Why, Tonton, what's the matter?

GASTON. Matter?

GIGI. Yes, you're blushing!

MME. ALVAREZ. *(From her position at the buffet, turns quickly to* GASTON's *rescue)* You mustn't make personal remarks, dear. Gaston, you'll have to forgive her.

GASTON. *(Moving up to* MME. ALVAREZ) Oh, that's all right. *(Goes to door, gets hat, coat, stick from hatrack, stands in doorway)* Dash it all! I don't know why I ever made that dinner date with the Feydeaus. I never hated leaving anything so much *(Quick look at* GIGI) —as that cassoulet of yours, Mamita.

(GIGI has stooped to floor, and is picking up cards, spilled in the tussle.)

MME. ALVAREZ. *(With a gracious bow)* In the name of my cassoulet, I thank you.

GASTON. Till I'm back from Switzerland—goodbye! *(Exits.)*

MME. ALVAREZ *and* GIGI. Goodbye!

MME. ALVAREZ. Come, Gigi, pick up your cards!

(She gets tablecloth from drawer of buffet, prepares to set table for supper, as ANDREE *enters with glass of camomile, with which she is gargling, crossing to stand front of sofa for "Figaro.")*

ANDREE. Oh—did Gaston leave? *(In hoarse whisper.)*

MME. ALVAREZ. Yes.

ANDREE. I'm so anxious to see whether this piece mentions the skating-teacher— Hm—looking Liane over, she's not so wonderful! Dahh!

MME. ALVAREZ. *(To above table, with knives and forks and plates, which she puts on table)* Oh she, she is! You talk like one of those scatterbrains who say I'd look just as well as Madame de Pougy, if I had a seven-strand collar of pearls! But success like theirs is never the result of luck—it's the result of discipline and careful training. Ask your Aunt Alicia! *(Putting last plate into place.)*

ANDREE. Well, everyone can't be as successful as Aunt Alicia.   *(WARN Curtain.)*

MME. ALVAREZ. But everyone can at least *try!*

GIGI. *(Having finally collected all the cards, rises)* Do you think Tonton will remember my music-roll, Grandma? He's so forgetful.

MME. ALVAREZ. Well, if he forgets any more, you can telephone him.

ANDREE *and* GIGI. *(Together)* Telephone!

GIGI. *(Rushing to* MME. ALVAREZ, *puts her arms around her)* Telephone! Telephone Tonton? Oh, Grandma, Grandma, Grandma!

ANDREE. *(Crossing to down Left of dining-table, and in a heavy hoarse voice)* When did you decide on a telephone, Maman?

MME. ALVAREZ. *(From above table)* Just now—today.

ANDREE. What made you *do* it?

MME. ALVAREZ. Because Gigi— *(Realizing what she is about to say)* —go wash the asparagus!

GIGI. I will, Grandma. *(Exits into kitchen.)*

MME. ALVAREZ. *(Calling off)* And don't forget your rubber gloves! *(Suddenly remembering one of the many essentials)* Soft, white hands are the first mark of a desirable woman.

GIGI. *(From kitchen)* I won't forget!

ANDREE. *(The height of her excitement)* A telephone— a telephone!

MME. ALVAREZ. *(Who has now brought a bottle of wine and corkscrew from buffet above table)* It's not to call up the Post and Telegraph—so don't *you* get excited! *(Proceds to remove cork from bottle.)*

ANDREE. *(Forgetting her hoarseness completely)* Oh— who's getting excited, Maman?*(Starts for bedroom door)* Now, if Monsieur Durand wants to get excited when he hears about it, let him go ahead and do it. After all, *he's* the excitable type, not I, Maman! *(As she goes through door, she sings excitedly)* A telephone—a telephone— a telephone—etc., etc., etc.

MME. ALVAREZ. *(By this time the wine is opened and left on the table. She brings long loaf of French bread from buffet, and slams it on table)* Oh—you squeaky canary!!

LIGHTS quickly dim, and the

CURTAIN FALLS

ACT TWO

SCENE I

SCENE: *As the Curtain rises, one can hear the ringing of the newly-installed TELEPHONE, which is on the wall just above the fireplace.*

Stage is empty, but presently, SIDONIE, Mme. Alvarez' combination maid, laundress, and garment-presser, bustles in from the kitchen. She starts to Right, then absentmindedly to the Left, but the ringing of the phone reminds her of its exact location.—She crosses to it, and apprehensively takes the receiver from the hook.

SIDONIE. *(None too familiar with apparatus, speaks gingerly into phone)* Allo!—allo! Who is this? Who?—Oh! Oh, Monsieur Lachaille! So you're back from Switzerland?—This is Sidonie, Monsieur! I'm Mme Alvarez's combination maid, scrubwoman, laundress, window-cleaner. You don't know me, because Madame generally rushes me out of here before noon.—you see, she pays me by the hour.—You do not know me, but I'm *dying* to meet you, Monsieur. I know all about you. You're the talk of the whole neighborhood.
(One ring of DOORBELL.)
The doorbell's ringing, Monsieur! I'll be right back, so don't go away! *(Another ring. She rests receiver carefully on back of armchair, and hurries to the door, muttering as she goes. Opens door)* Oh, *you!*
VICTOR. Hello, old dear!
SIDONIE. Well, come on in! *(She starts back to phone)* I'm talking to Monsieur Lachaille on the telephone!

45

VICTOR. *(Entering with wicker basket containing four quarts and two pints of champagne, which he places on dining-table)* That ought to give him a thrill! *(Sits Right of table.)*

SIDONIE. *(Back at phone)* Well, here I am again, Monsieur!—No, Monsieur, Mme Alvarez is out, but she will be back soon—she went to fetch Mademoiselle Gigi from school— Oh, she is getting so strict with the poor child these days.—Yes, Monsieur?—Shall I put the kettle on for camomile? *(Getting her usual bright idea, gives a look to the basket of champagne)* Or will you drink champagne?—Yes!—yes!—yes!—yes! Yes, that is what I said, Monsieur—*Champagne!* It arrived this very moment, from Madame Alicia!—Ohhh, yes, Monsieur! Very well, Monsieur.—Goodbye, Monsieur! *(She fairly moans this farewell into the receiver, hangs up, and pantomimes kiss to the telephone. Then starts for the kitchen)* Champagne! What next!?

VICTOR. Well, I hope there's nothing more coming over here for a little while!

SIDONIE. *(Returning from kitchen, puts several pieces of silverware on buffet, and goes to above table; proceeds to open basket and remove champagne bottles from their straw covers)* What a spoiled housecat you are!

VICTOR. Now wait a moment! What about all that stuff last week?

SIDONIE. A couple of baskets of china? And some silver?

VICTOR. And cases of pate de foie gras—and anchovies! Well, I must say, the little one is being launched with all the trimmings!

SIDONIE. I don't know what you're talking about!

VICTOR. You don't, eh? Those cars of Lachaille's are a little conspicuous, standing out in front of this tenement, my little cabbage!

SIDONIE. Monsieur Lachaille has paid regular calls on us for years. Madame Alvarez is like a mother to him.

VICTOR. And since when has he been sending expensive presents to the Little One?

SIDONIE. What's so terrific about a music-roll for a school-girl?

VICTOR. A school-girl, eh? Ha! They tell me it's got silver clasps.

SIDONIE. Oh, gossiping with the concierge, eh?

VICTOR. Well, all I've got to say is, I'm sorry for Lachaille!

SIDONIE. Sorry for Monsieur Lachaille! Why, all his life, he's been sitting in a tub full of butter, with a great big silver spoon in his mouth!

VICTOR. And how comfortable do you think that is? To sit in a greasy tub, with a big spoon in your mouth?

SIDONIE. Ohhh,—*you! (Takes three bottles into the kitchen.)*

VICTOR. I'm serious! My brother spent years in the service of the Lachaille family. Why, before he even started shaving, every woman in Paris was trying to dip into that sugar bin of his!

(SIDONIE enters, gets remaining bottles, and takes them to the kitchen.)

And for him to be shorn *now,* by a pupil of Madame Alicia! Any time the little one falters, her Aunt will step in and help! Clip! Clip!

(SIDONIE exits to kitchen.)

I've a good mind to tip him off—

(One ring, DOORBELL.)

to their whole game before it's too late!

SIDONIE. *(Enters)* Shhhh! *(Opens front door.)*

GIGI. *(Enters, carrying an elaborate Russian-leather music-roll with silver clasps. Her mood might be called one of dreamy dignity)* Good afternoon, Victor! *(She crosses down Left, puts roll on stand front of settee, gets atlas, drawing-pad, compass, and GASTON'S cigarette case from down stage end of piano—takes them to stand— sits on sofa, and proceeds to do her school-work.)*

VICTOR. *(Rising, crossing down stage a few steps)* Good afternoon, Mademoiselle. I've just brought over some champagne to go with the foie gras.

GIGI. *(Preoccupied)* Really?

SIDONIE. *(Dropping down stage a few steps)* Didn't your grandma pick you up at school?

GIGI. Yes, but she stopped downstairs, to finish the marketing.

VICTOR. Is there any message for your Aunt, Mademoiselle?

GIGI. No, thanks.

(SIDONIE *and* VICTOR *exchange a knowing look. She steps a bit closer to* GIGI.)

SIDONIE. Do you want Victor to tell her that Monsieur Lachaille is back?

GIGI. *(With a little start)* He's back? Tonton?

(VICTOR *moves up to table, and gets wicker basket, preparatory to leaving.)*

SIDONIE. I've just been talking to him on the apparatus. He said he'd be right over.

GIGI. How did he know we had a telephone?

SIDONIE. Your Grandma wrote him about it.

GIGI. I see— *(To* VICTOR, *who has crossed down Center two or three steps, with basket)* You may tell my aunt about Monsieur Lachaille, Victor.

VICTOR. Very well, Mademoiselle. *(Starts to go.)* Goodbye!

SIDONIE. Shouldn't you put your new dress on, Mademoiselle—Goodbye, Victor!—for the company?

(VICTOR *exits front door.)*

GIGI. There's no hurry. Aunty says it's better to make a late entrance anyway.

(SIDONIE *goes to buffet, gets silverware, polish, and rag, sits Right of dining-table and begins to work.)*
To think that he came back from his holiday ahead of time!

SIDONIE. I had a feeling he might, all along.

GIGI. You felt that, too, Sidonie?

SIDONIE. Definitely! I felt it, when he began to delay his trip, in order to *bring* you the music-roll, instead of having it sent from the shop.

GIGI. The music-roll, plus two dozen boxes of licorice —twenty-four boxes of rat-tails!

SIDONIE. Yes, the only mystery is, why he went away at *all*.

GIGI. To get away from Liane.

SIDONIE. Did he tell you that?

GIGI. Of course not. He didn't have to tell me. *(Puts down compass, and picks up music-roll)* It's the most expensive music-roll in Paris, Sidonie! *(Holds it fondly)* These silver clasps weigh a ton. It cost so much, it's actually in bad taste—and you know how careful Monsieur Lachaille is about money!

SIDONIE. That's right! Why, last year he never *did* produce the sugar for your grandma's jam. And this very month, he was so careless, that he sent it twice!—How he has changed, that man!

GIGI. He really has. Why, he'd never taken dinner here, until that evening Grandma made the cassoulet with the goose he sent us. Do you realize that, Sidonie?

SIDONIE. I realized it—washing all those dishes the next morning!

GIGI. *(Putting down music-roll, and picking up cigarette-case)* And what a dinner party it was! How Tonton laughed, when I told him I copied my whole examination from the girl at the next desk and then found out she had it all wrong! *(Excitedly, she runs to chair Left of dining-table, jumps on it, and sits on the back)* Don't you think that's funny, Sidonie?

SIDONIE. Well—medium funny, perhaps.

GIGI. Why, Tonton and I both roared, until the tears ran down our cheeks. And after dinner, Maman drank too much champagne, and insisted on singing the Bell Song from Lakme. Did *you* ever hear her sing it, Sidonie?

SIDONIE. Alas!—who hasn't?

GIGI. But Tonton would have sat and listened like a

little lamb, if Grandma hadn't bustled Maman off to bed, *(Indicating cigarette-case)* And then I won this from him at piquet. *(She gives it a rub on the sleeves of her dress, breathes on it, and any other means of polishing)* Of course he had to make that joke of his, about me cheating. But he gave it up, almost without a whimper. So I've been taking it to school every day, filled with rat-tails. I pass them around, just carelessly, *(Reaching, gets polishing-rag from* SIDONIE, *rubs case)* —as if a gold case, set with precious stones were nothing at all!
          *(*SIDONIE *regains her cloth.)*
But what an absolute sensation, Sidonie—when I said I won it from Monsieur Lachaille—the notorious man-about-town and gambler!

          (Tosses case to SIDONIE, *who catches it.)*

SIDONIE. *(Inspecting the case)* Gambler!—I didn't know Monsieur was a gambler!
GIGI. Oh, he isn't! But it gives a wrong impression about Tonton, when you tell the truth. People can't realize how wonderful he really is, unless you lie about him.
SIDONIE. I know—I felt that way myself once, about a very exceptional plumber.
GIGI. You did, Sidonie? What happened to him?
SIDONIE. Oh, he disappeared—as I grew older.
GIGI. Too bad.
SIDONIE. Yes. You're going to find out everyone grows older, Mademoiselle Gigi. *(Returns case to her.)*
GIGI. I've found that out already. I realized it, when Grandma and I were in the fitting-room at Paquin's, and Madame Henriette pinned my hair up for the first time, so that it wouldn't interfere with the high collar. *(Lifting her hair, to give the effect to* SIDONIE*)* Have you seen that collar, Sidonie? *(Drops into seat of chair.)*
SIDONIE. How can I—when your Grandma has got the whole outfit pinned up tight in a sheet!
GIGI. *(Lost in enthusiasm)* Well, it's made of genuine imitation Venise lace, with whalebones that come up clear behind my ears— *(Indicates this.)*

SIDONIE. *(Joining in her excitement)* They do?

GIGI. *(Rising to above table, near* SIDONIE*)* And the bodice is tight—tight, with a belt made of grosgrain, that has an enormous gold buckle. And the sleeves are leg of mutton and perfectly enormous, and the skirt is yellow striped silk, with six frilly petticoats that rustle like a railroad train!

SIDONIE. *(Beside herself)* Six of them! Tsch! Tsch! Tsch!

GIGI. *(Crossing down Left, gets fan out of music-roll)* And to give me something to do with my hands, Aunty has loaned me one of her own ivory-handled fans! *(Drops into sofa, slightly fatigued.)*

SIDONIE. *(Gathering up her silver and polish, rises)* How elegant! You'll end up covered in jewels—like Mademoiselle Liane!

GIGI. Oh!—do you think I will, Sidonie?

SIDONIE. Yes, indeed! You're going to be a real credit to your family. *(Crosses up Right, replaces polish on sideboard.)*

(ANDREE *enters from bedroom, in dressing-gown. She carries in her hand the part for the new operetta.)*

GIGI. Good afternoon, Maman.

ANDREE. *(Kissing* GIGI's *forehead, sighs wearily)* Good afternoon, dear.

GIGI. What's the matter? Didn't you rest well?

ANDREE. *(Crossing to sit on pouffe Center)* Not at all! I'm so dull today—I just can't seem to learn this new part.

SIDONIE. *(Moving down Right of* ANDREE*)* There's some champagne in the kitchen, that was sent over by your Aunt, Madame—

ANDREE. *(At once interested)* Champagne?

SIDONIE. It might sharpen your wits to have a drop—

ANDREE. Yes, Sidonie—!

SIDONIE. But of course, to open a bottle without Madame Alvarez's permission— Oh, la, la!

ANDREE. Perhaps a pint bottle— *(Quick look to* GIGI, *and back to* SIDONIE) —if there *is* one—

SIDONIE. There are two pints!

ANDREE. Wouldn't *my* permission do—if it's only a pint, Sidonie?

SIDONIE. Well, let's stretch a point, and *try* it, anyway! *(She hurries off to the kitchen.)*

ANDREE. *(Makes a feeble attempt to study her part)* Oh dear! This new role is very tricky!

GIGI. *(Who has been busy with her compass and atlas)* Would it help, if I read cues for you, Maman?

ANDREE. That would be sweet of you, darling. *(Rises, crossing above stand; gives part to* GIGI, *indicates the right line)* Go alone. *(She returns to the pouffe, sits.)*

GIGI. *(Reading from script)* Will you let Her Highness go alone?

ANDREE. *(Sings prolonged note, the lyric of which is)* No!

GIGI. *(Curling up on sofa)* Are you aware the Prince is with her?

ANDREE. *(Singing long note)* No! *(Slight cough and clearing throat.)*

GIGI. Do you think they will be married?

ANDREE. *(Short, staccato note)* No!

GIGI. Would the citizens dare attack them?

(After a count of three, POP of champagne cork is heard from kitchen, causing ANDREE *to forget the business at hand. She looks toward kitchen.)*

Maman!

ANDREE. *(Coming to attention)* Oh, beg pardon, dear.

GIGI. Would the citizens dare attack them?

ANDREE. *(Having trouble thinking of correct answer,—* GIGI *attempts to help her)* No, don't prompt me! *(Still struggling for answer, rises, crosses to Right—suddenly remembering, turns to* GIGI) No!

MME. ALVAREZ. *(At which point,* MME. ALVAREZ *enters from the front door with daily provisions)* Gigi, dear! You're not getting ready, with Gaston on his way here! *(Puts things on dining-table.)*

GIGI. How did you know, Grandma?

MME. ALVAREZ. The concierge. He heard it from Victor. Go get into your new dress. Hurry, hurry, hurry!

(GIGI *exits to bedroom.*)

Well, Andree—it's easy to see you're in no danger of being seen by anyone important.

(SIDONIE *enters with tumbler of champagne. She silently steals above* MME. ALVAREZ, *so as not to be seen.*)

(*Crossing up to hatrack, removes hat and boa*) A distinguished admirer around the place would soon cure you of a robe and bedroom slippers.

(*During this,* SIDONIE, *still unobserved by* MME. ALVAREZ, *has crossed down Right of table, to above* ANDREE *at down Right.*)

ANDREE. (*Quietly singing*) No—no—no! (*Turns to* MME. ALVAREZ) Yes, Maman!

(SIDONIE *hands her the glass of champagne, and* ANDREE *continues.*)

Thanks, Sidonie!

MME. ALVAREZ. (*Has crossed down Left of table, to Left Center, sees* ANDREE *take the glass from* SIDONIE) What is that?

SIDONIE. Pommery, 1882, Madame.

MME. ALVAREZ. Champagne?

SIDONIE. Yes, Madame. Sent over by Madame Alicia.

MME. ALVAREZ. I see. (*Takes three threatening steps toward* SIDONIE) That wine was sent here for the sole purpose of entertaining M. Lachaille.

SIDONIE. Yes, Madame Alvarez. (*Reaches to* ANDREE *for glass*) If you please, Madame.

MME. ALVAREZ. Never mind—since you've opened it. But from now on, orders for champagne will come from nobody but *me*.

SIDONIE. Yes, Madame.

ANDREE. (*Having taken a sip of champagne*) Maman, do you suppose the rumor's true that Liane has followed Gaston to Switzerland?

MME. ALVAREZ. Where did you ever hear any such story?

ANDREE. Last night, at the theater.

(During this, SIDONIE'S *head turns from* MME. ALVAREZ *to* ANDREE *and back again, trying to collect as much gossip as possible.)*

MME. ALVAREZ. And only *now* you tell me?

ANDREE. Well, what difference does it make?

MME. ALVAREZ. Not the least bit in the whole world, dear—to *you.* *(Suddenly becoming conscious of* SIDONIE'S *presence)* Does this interest *you?*

SIDONIE. Yes, Madame—no, Madame!

MME. ALVAREZ. Then take those things to the kitchen, and get out of here!

SIDONIE. Yes, Madame. *(Crosses up Right of table, picks up shopping-bag, starts for kitchen. Drops bag on floor.)*

MME. ALVAREZ. *(Who has crossed to front of sofa)* Look out—those eggs! *(She sits.)*

SIDONIE. *(Picking up bag.* ANDREE *crosses, puts glass on stand front of sofa, sits on pouffe, looking at her libretto)* Perhaps with company coming, it would be good for me to stay and serve the refreshments?

ALVAREZ. Risk my sister's priceless china in those butter-fingers?

SIDONIE. But I will be careful, and it would lend a touch of elegance.

MME. ALVAREZ. All right, Sidonie.

(SIDONIE *exits into kitchen.* ANDREE *is practicing her "No—no—no's.")*

That woman has been waiting for a chance like this for years.

ANDREE. *(Still practicing)* No—no—no!

MME. ALVAREZ. But you *know* she has! Will you please stop studying that two-letter word you've got to learn, and listen to me?

ANDREE. All right, Maman—what is it?

MME. ALVAREZ. Did anyone say whether or not Liane made up with Gaston in Switzerland?

ANDREE. The opinions last night were divided. Some said "yes" and some said "no." *(Starts to sing the word no—but catches herself in time.)*

MME. ALVAREZ. Oh dear, if it had happened here in Paris, the whole business would be in all the papers, but how can anyone tell about anything, 'way off in those Alps?

ANDREE. Do *you* think she's made up with him, Maman?

MME. ALVAREZ. I don't know *what* to think—if I could only talk to Alicia.

ANDREE. But, Maman—you *can*. *(As MME. ALVAREZ looks at her, she indicates the telephone.)*

MME. ALVAREZ. Oh—of course. *(Rises, and crosses to phone.)*

ANDREE. Who's stupid now, Maman dear? *(Starts singing melody of Bell Song, softly.)*

MME. ALVAREZ. *(At phone)* Hello?—will you give me number three hundred and twenty-seven, please. I want three hundred twenty-seven.

(ANDREE has increased in volume.)

Are you going to put on a dress, before Gaston gets here?

(ANDREE'S singing increases, and MME ALVAREZ tries to top her.)

Are *you* going to put on a dress,—

(ANDREE stops. MME. ALVAREZ returns to normal voice.)

—before Gaston gets here?

ANDREE. Oh well— *(Rises)* —I suppose I'll have to. *(Crosses to bedroom door.)*

MME. ALVAREZ. And while I think of it, we'll do very well this afternoon without the Bell Song from Lakme.

ANDREE. *(Stopping in door)* Maman!—you know I never sing without an invitation.

MME. ALVAREZ. And see you don't open any more of that champagne. *(Into phone)* Hello—hello!

(ANDREE, being reminded of champagne, sneaks

into kitchen while MME. ALVAREZ' *back is turned,
returns with quart of champagne, and exits into the
bedroom, closing the door after her.)*

(MME. ALVAREZ *speaks into the phone during the above)*
Hello? This is Madame Alvarez. I'd like to talk to my
sister, please.—Hello, Alicia? I think you had best come
over.—He just called up—just now. He's on his way here
—the rumor is that Liane followed him to Switzerland—
Oh, I can chaperone Gilberte, of course, but in case that
woman has actually been— *(Lowers her voice)* —been
with him, it's going to need— *(Sound of champagne
POP, off in bedroom.* MME. ALVAREZ *stops, not quite
sure of what she has heard, pauses, decides to continue
her conversation)* —to need the sort of delicate treat-
ment, which only *you* can supply.
    (Sound of GASTON'S *three rings of the DOOR-
    BELL.)*
He's at the door this moment—so hurry dear. Goodbye.
    (DOORBELL rings.)
Sidonie! Didn't you hear the bell?

(There is a CRASH of broken dishes, off in the kitchen.)

    SIDONIE. *(From offstage)* Yes, Madame, I'm coming!
(Enters carrying two pieces of broken plate.)
    MME. ALVAREZ. *(Crossing to Right of dining-table)*
Now what?
    SIDONIE. *(To above table)* It can be mended, Madame.
I've broken things into far smaller pieces than this!
    MME. ALVAREZ. Wait a moment! Give me that!
    (DOORBELL rings.)
*(Takes plate from her, looks about for place to hide it,
and finally puts it on floor under draperies at Right of
arch.)*
    SIDONIE. *(Starting to front doorway, but stopping to
arrange her hair in hall-rack mirror)* Just a minute,
Monsieur—I am coming—I am coming!
    MME. ALVAREZ. *(Simultaneously crossing to bedroom
door, and calling to* ANDREE) Andree— Gaston is here—
are you presentable?

(By this time, SIDONIE has opened the door, and GASTON enters. MME. ALVAREZ crosses quickly to Left of arch, to greet him.)

SIDONIE. *(Opening door)* Well, M. Lachaille!

(GASTON, crossing down to MME. ALVAREZ at Left Center.)

GASTON. Good afternoon.

SIDONIE. *(Following down, trying to fit herself in between MME. ALVAREZ and GASTON)* I am Sidonie, Monsieur—I am Sidonie!

MME. ALVAREZ. Gaston, my dear—welcome back from your voyage!

GASTON. Mamita! *(Hands her a bouquet of flowers which he has brought with him.)*

MME. ALVAREZ. You're looking wonderful. *(Takes flowers)* And flowers for Gilberte! How chic! *(Bows slightly to him.)*

GASTON. But those are for *you*, Mamita.

MME. ALVAREZ. For me? How nice!

(Offers her Right hand to him; he kisses it.)

GASTON. *(Reaches into his pocket, takes out a rubber ball with a string attached to it, bounces it on floor)* I brought *this* for Gigi.

MME. ALVAREZ. *(Reacting quickly enough to avoid being hit by ball)* Oh!—oh! Well, she'll be—delighted. *(Handing flowers to SIDONIE)* Sidonie, you may put these in water—and—

(SIDONE inhales deeply their perfume, with a roll of the eye toward GASTON.)

—and bring in some champagne—with champagne glasses!

SIDONIE. I know, the ones with the long legs. *(Exits to kitchen.)*

MME. ALVAREZ. *(A few steps toward sofa)* Well, Gaston,—so you just got back?

GASTON. *(Following down)* Oh no, I've been back for several days.

MME. ALVAREZ. You have? And you never got in touch with us?

GASTON. Well, I've been busy, Mamita. *(Bounces ball)* I took your advice about seeing a lot of my young friends.

MME. ALVAREZ. Oh? *(Sits on sofa.)*

GASTON. I gave a really bang-up party at the Pre-Catelan last Thursday night.

MME. ALVAREZ. But the Pre Catelan isn't open yet.

GASTON. I got them to open up, fifteen days ahead of time. *(Bounces ball.)*

MME. ALVAREZ. Gaston! But what extravagance!

GASTON. *(Sitting on pouffe)* Yes, it did cost a rather pretty penny. I hired Footit and Chocolat to do a turn between courses.

MME. ALVAREZ. Really?

GASTON. A strange little dwarf, named Count Lautrec, got tight, and was very amusing. But the grand finale was the big thing. Rita del Erido, from the Hippodrome, rode right in between tables on horseback, *(Imitating the rider)* —in a stunning silver riding-habit, all trimmed with ostrich plumes.

MME. ALVAREZ. But we never read a *word* about all of this!

GASTON. Oh, I've learned a thing or two about publicity. I let *Gil Blas* know I'd withdraw the subsidy I granted them, if they ever mentioned a word about it.

MME. ALVAREZ. I see.

GASTON. I bought Del Erido a lavalliere, Mamita— bigger than the one I gave Liane last Christmas.

MME. ALVAREZ. Gaston! Why, I've never heard of you spending money like that.

GASTON. Oh well—one only lives once! *(Bounces the ball.)*

MME. ALVAREZ. *(After slight pause)* Something's changed you, Gaston.

GASTON. *(Rising)* Something *has* changed me, Mamita. I don't know myself. I've never been like this in my whole life. Maybe it's nerves. *(Crosses to down Right playing extravagantly with the ball)* I keep wanting to do something absolutely outrageous, and then when I do it, it seems dull. *(Crossing back to Center)* I wasn't even impressed by the Matterhorn!

MME. ALVAREZ. Gaston, there's a rumour around Paris, that Liane followed you to Switzerland.

GASTON. *(Quietly)* Do people say she did?

MME. ALVAREZ. Then she didn't?

GASTON. *(Dejectedly putting one foot on pouffe, and resting his arm on his knee)* No. It was blasted lonely there at Lucerne. *(Trying to assume a cheerful air)* What a woman she is—that Del Erido! *(Removing his foot from pouffe)* Why, her figure begins where Liane's leaves off!

MME. ALVAREZ. You're not thinking of del Erido, Gaston. You're thinking of Liane.

GASTON. *(In front of pouffe)* Is that what this is, Mamita?

MME. ALVAREZ. I'm afraid so.

GASTON. *(Suddenly sits on pouffe. As he covers his face with his hands, the ball dangles and bounces on its elastic string, which GASTON holds in his hand)* Mamita! You know everything!

MME. ALVAREZ. *(Rises, to above him, tries to console him)* Poor boy! Poor boy! What are you going to do about her?

GASTON. Nothing. I have my pride. There's nothing in Heaven or earth, that would make me take her back.

MME. ALVAREZ. I only hope you're going to stick to that!

SIDONIE. *(Has entered, with silver tray, on which are three champagne glasses, and one quart of champagne. She comes to up stage end of sofa)* What's the matter, Madame? Does our company feel sick?

(GASTON recovers himself quickly, and rises. MME. ALVAREZ crosses two steps toward SIDONIE.)

MME. ALVAREZ. You may serve—in silence! *(Crosses, sits sofa.)*

SIDONIE. Oh yes, Madame. *(Crosses to dining-table.)*

GASTON. *(Glad of an occupation, goes to* SIDONIE*)* Here—let me open that bottle for you.

ANDREE. *(Enters from bedroom, still in negligee, and feeling the effect of her champagne; crosses behind sofa, to* GASTON. *She has empty glass with her)* Well, well, Gaston! Good afternoon! *(Slightly loses control of her balance as she shakes hands with* GASTON.*)*

GASTON. Andree, my dear! How goes it?

ANDREE. *(Doing her best at being the lady)* Very—very—well! *(Crosses and drops in chair Right, by fireplace. Sits on knitting-needles, which she lightly tosses to floor.)*

GASTON. And how is the Little One?

ANDREE. *(Having a little speech trouble)* Gi-Gi-Gi—is getting to be rather moody these days. *(Her arm slips from side chair, she replaces it)* Haven't you noticed it, Maman?

MME. ALVAREZ. *(Staring at her)* Not particularly!

ANDREE. I think it's the way the child gourmandizes. If Gigi's brains were as active as her jaws, she might begin to show some sense—

(Pleased with herself, she starts to laugh. GASTON *opens champagne. POP. This sound halts* ANDREE, *then she continues her laugh—this time in a higher key.)*

SIDONIE. I'll pass the champagne around, Monsieur. That is what I am here for. Please sit down!

*(*GASTON *finishes pouring three glasses of champagne, and sits on pouffe, lights cigarette.* SIDONIE *takes tray to* MME ALVAREZ, *and gives her glass.)*

ANDREE. *(With still a bit too much over-projection of her words)* I meant to tell you, Maman, that Gigi should stop eating those garlic sausages—

(SIDONIE *has crossed above* GASTON, *to the Right
of him. At this point,* ANDREE *holds out her glass
to* SIDONIE, *who takes it quickly from her, and offers
tray to* GASTON.)

She had a pimple last week, right on her nose.

(GASTON *takes glass, and he and* MME ALVAREZ *drink.*
SIDONIE *takes a few steps toward kitchen, and
drains the third glass which is left on her tray.*)

MME. ALVAREZ. Andree!

SIDONIE. *(Turning back to* MME. ALVAREZ) Oh yes,
she did, Madame. It was I, myself, who warned Mademoiselle not to squeeze it.

ANDREE. *(During this,* ANDREE *has been trying to indicate the location of said pimple, by grabbing her own
nose—with luck, she finally makes it)* Well—make her
listen to you, Sidonie, the next time.

SIDONIE. Yes, Madame. *(Exits to kitchen.)*

MME. ALVAREZ. Andree!

ANDREE. (ANDREE, *rising to Right of* GASTON) I
smelled her breath last evening, but it was right after
dinner, so I couldn't tell about it.

MME. ALVAREZ. Gaston is not interested in your clin-
ical observations.

ANDREE. *(Giving* GASTON *a playful push)* Oh, Gaston
knows about children. You've got nieces in the family,
haven't you?

GASTON. *(Recovering himself)* Yes, of course.

ANDREE. I'm going to buy the child a bottle of Cascara
today. I'm sure she doesn't go regularly enough to the—

MME. ALVAREZ. That will *do!*

(GIGI *enters from bedroom. She is wearing her dress from
Paquin, and carries the fan given her by her* AUNT
ALICIA. *In her best lady-like fashion, she crosses to
down stage end of sofa, makes a complete turn, as*
GASTON, *speechless for the moment, gazes at her.*)

GIGI. Well, Tonton? *(Starts to cross in front of him to down Right)* Why, what's the matter?

GASTON. *(His eyes following her)* Matter?

MME. ALVAREZ. *(Jumping in)* Gaston has neglected us so long, dear, he doesn't recognize you any more.

(ANDREE moves to above dining-table, watching GIGI, whose enthusiasm now breaks through her efforts to be elegant,—she whirls to Right of GASTON.)

GIGI. Look, Tonton! My skirt is four metres and twenty-five around. And that isn't all! I've got a box-coat, just like Mlle. de Merode's. And two new hats, and another pair of high-heeled shoes. *(Strikes a pose and curtsies)* Well—what do you think of me?

GASTON. You look exactly like an organ-grinder's monkey!

MME. ALVAREZ. Gaston!

ANDREE. (ANDREE, *attempting to hit table with her hand, misses it, and lunges forward)* I side with you, Gaston! You're absolutely right!

(GASTON, rising, puts his half-empty glass on dining-table, and goes to GIGI at Right. ANDREE immediately picks up unfinished drink left by GASTON.)

GASTON. You see? Your mother knows! Come over here! *(Takes GIGI by the arm, holds her in front of him, and makes her look in the mirror)* That collar makes you look just like a hen that's eaten too many chick-peas!

GIGI. Tonton!

GASTON. *(Two steps back from her)* I liked you a lot better, in your old blue dress!

(ANDREE, sipping drink, moves slowly around Left end of table, to front of it.)

GIGI. You pretend to know a lot of things, Tonton, but I never heard of your having any taste in dress!

GASTON. Now really!

(ANDREE *breaks into the Bell Song, rests glass on top of her head. She moves to* GASTON, *and dances with a furious motion of the hips.* MME. ALVAREZ, *seeing that* ANDREE *is completely out of control, crosses to her and grabs her by the left arm, and struggles to get her off into the bedroom. Hearing the noise,* SIDONIE *enters from kitchen, takes in the situation.*)

SIDONIE. Well, here we go!

MME. ALVAREZ. (*Pulling* ANDREE, *who is still singing and wiggling all the while*) That's enough! We've seen everything we want!

(*The DOORBELL rings furiously.* SIDONIE *starts for door, but* MME. ALVAREZ, *who has now succeeded in pushing the still-singing* ANDREE *into the bedroom, starts to answer the door. DOORBELL.*)

Never mind, Sidonie; I'll answer it!

(SIDONIE *exits into kitchen.* MME. ALVAREZ *pauses for a second, to get her breath, then opens the door. During this,* GIGI, *at the point of tears, sits in the armchair by the fireplace, her back to the whole scene.* GASTON *is above the chair, pretty amazed by the whole performance.* ALICIA *enters.* MME. AL-VAREZ *kisses* ALICIA *on the cheek.*)

Alicia!

ALICIA. Inez, my dear! (*Crossing down Right of table, to* GASTON) Gaston! How well you look, my boy.

(GIGI *rises, stands front of armchair.*)

GASTON. (*Kissing her hand*) Madame!

ALICIA. A little bit thin, perhaps, but it only brings out those fatal eyes of yours. Gilberte! Is that a new dress I see?

(MME. ALVAREZ *has moved down to up stage end of sofa.*)

GIGI. Yes, Aunty.

ALICIA. *(Moving to her)* My child, what's wrong? What is it?

GIGI. Tonton doesn't like my dress. He says—he says —I look like a monkey! *(Bursts into big cry.)*

ALICIA. *(Consoling her)* Dear, dear!

(GIGI *moves up to* ALICIA.)

GASTON. *(To Left of* ALICIA) I didn't mean it that way, Madame! I was joking. Please don't cry, Gigi. *(Gets ball from pocket)* Look · what I've brought you! *(Dangles ball on elastic string)* I got it at the railroad station in Lucerne.

GIGI. *(With bitter sarcasm, as she takes the ball)* That's nice of you—that's just too awfully—dreadfully nice! *(Violently throws the ball at* GASTON.)

GASTON. *(Outraged)* Oh, I say now!!

ALICIA. Gilberte! What manners!

GIGI. Well, what kind of manners has *he* got—calling me a monkey!? *(Crosses to* GASTON, *pushing him in chest.* GASTON *backs to Center, front of dining-table.)* And what do you think *you* look like, Monsieur Lachaille? *(Another push)* That famous cook who belonged to the Prince of Wales can't be feeding you very well! You've gotten so scrawny, your nose looks perfectly enormous! *(Pushes his nose upward.)*

MME. ALVAREZ. Go to your room, Gigi!!

GIGI. *(Angrily, running to bedroom, exits)* All right, Grandma!

GASTON. *(Shakes his head, as though it had been dislocated—in general pulling himself together; steps down stage and faces* MME. ALVAREZ) Well, Mamita! You have my compliments! A fine bringing-up you've given that child! *(Starts for front door, via Right of table, and bumps into chair; pulls himself together, and exits with as much dignity as remains.)*

ALICIA. *(A few steps to Center)* In the name of Heaven, what's come over Gilberte?

MME. ALVAREZ. *(Shrugs her shoulders)* I don't know; she's never behaved like this in her whole life.

ALICIA. Well, Lachaille is right—it looks as if you'd brought her up to be a savage.

MME. ALVAREZ. And what about *him?* Leaving here in a blind fury?

ALICIA. Exactly. In a state where he could go right off to Liane!

MME. ALVAREZ. Nonsense! He told me just now that nothing in Heaven or earth could ever make him take her back.

ALICIA. It's as bad as that, eh?

MME. ALVAREZ. Bad?

ALICIA. Such a statement only proves that the woman is still under his skin. And furthermore, he's not dealing with an amateur. *(Takes paper clipping from her muff)* I just tore this out of the afternoon paper— Mademoiselle Liane has committed suicide!

MME. ALVAREZ. *(Moving in to* ALICIA*)* Is she dead this time?

ALICIA. Certainly not!

MME. ALVAREZ. What did she use?

ALICIA. Laudanum, of course—as usual. Listen to this: *(She reads)* Without being able to give a definite statement as to the condition of the beautiful and desperate young creature, the doctors have given a favorable diagnosis.

MME. ALVAREZ. *My* diagnosis is, that she's going to get gunny-sacks under her eyes, from all those doses of laudanum!

ALICIA. But it's not *she* who is the interesting party. It's Lachaille. This is the first time it's ever happened to him. He's had all the other experiences, but Liane is his first suicide. I've no doubt in the world she'll make him feel all puffed up over it—while Gilberte spends her time insulting the man. *(Few steps to down Right.)*

MME. ALVAREZ. Well, Alicia—the project of launching Gigi is no easy thing!

ALICIA. *(Crossing back to* MME. ALVAREZ *at Center)*

Yes, I know—I'm beginning to think Gilberte should come and stay with *me*.

MME. ALVAREZ. Oh. *No*, Alicia!

ALICIA. And what's so offensive about staying with me?

MME. ALVAREZ. I didn't mean it like that— But Gigi is so used to the way *we* live—simply, and without elegance.

ALICIA. Do you want her to stay on *here*, where her mother frightens off anyone civilized? Where she'll fall in love with the rent-collector some day?—or the postman?

MME. ALVAREZ. Heaven forbid, Alicia—but your house would be much further from her school.

ALICIA. School, eh? She's already learned too much! I'm graduating her, right here and now!

MME. ALVAREZ. *(Resigned)* Well, I suppose you're right, as usual.

ALICIA. Then you may pack up the child's little bits and pieces, and I'll send over for her in the morning.

MME. ALVAREZ. All right. *(Looking away.)*

ALICIA. What's the matter?

MME. ALVAREZ. *(Looks toward bedroom door)* I just don't know how to get along without my Gigi, that's all.

ALICIA. *(Softening a little)* You'll have to get along without her, once she's launched, Inez. I'm afraid we both will. But that's the way things go, in this life.

(The DOORBELL rings, with the three short rings of GASTON.)

MME. ALVAREZ. Why, that's Gaston's ring!

ALICIA. Well, aren't you going to let the man in?

MME. ALVAREZ. Yes,—of course.

(Quickly goes to the door, opens it for GASTON, who enters, down Left of table, to Center.)

GASTON. Aren't I an idiot? I forgot my hat!

MME. ALVAREZ. *(Following down to Left of him)* Oh, did you, Gaston?

GASTON. I thought I'd take Gigi along to the Pre-Catelan, and buy her an ice.

ALICIA. To the Pre-Catelon?

GASTON. *(Turning to* MME. ALVAREZ) Yes,—may I?

MME. ALVAREZ. I don't see why not— *(Is suddenly stopped by sharp look from* ALICIA.)

ALICIA. Gaston! You know how fond of you we both are. But Inez and I must not forget that we're in charge of a young girl's future. For many years now, you've been coming here, playing with Gilberte, bringing her candy and toys. She swears by her Tonton. But whether you realize it or not, dear boy, things have changed. Gilberte is no longer a child.

GASTON. Why, she's only fifteen.

ALICIA. Over *sixteen!*

GASTON. That's right—she had a birthday!

ALICIA. And you want to take her to the Pre-Catelon in your motor car!

GASTON. Oh, Madame, you'll never make me believe I could compromise a slip of a girl like Gigi—a green weed —a child whom nobody knows or even looks at!

ALICIA. *(Two steps to the Right)* Whom nobody ever *has* looked at, Gaston! Her grown-up clothes may make her appear like a monkey in *your* eyes, but I assure you, my dear boy, if she were seen with you on the terrace of the Pre-Catelon, she would not only be noticed, but very much admired.

GASTON. Then why don't you come along and chaperone us?

ALICIA. Me? With my reputation as a grande cocotte? Why, people might think I was putting the child on the market!

MME. ALVAREZ. Which would never do, Gaston.

ALICIA. No, Gaston; before Gilberte ever sets foot into the great world, of which she will be such an exceptional ornament, she must enter into a formal liaison with some nice man, who will ensure her future.

GASTON. But, Madame—

ALICIA. I'm sure you understand. *(Crosses to him, extends her hand)* And now, I must go.

MME. ALVAREZ. I'll call Gilberte. *(Crosses behind sofa, to bedroom door)* Oh, Gigi! Come in, dear—your Aunt is leaving.

GIGI'S VOICE. What is it now? *(She enters to lower end of sofa, as MME. ALVAREZ returns to up stage end of sofa. GIGI has changed to her old dress)* Oh, did you come back?

GASTON. Yes—for my hat.

ALICIA. *(Crossing down to GIGI)* Oh, so we're not chic any more, dear, are we?

GIGI. No, Aunty.

ALICIA. Well, there's plenty of time for you to dazzle Paris. Goodbye Gilberte.

GIGI. Goodbye.

ALICIA. And do cheer up! You're going to come and stay with me.

GIGI. Am I?

ALICIA. Yes, a nice, long visit. *(Crosses up to Left of GASTON)* Goodbye, Gaston. *(Crossing up to doorway.)*

(MME. ALVAREZ follows to Left of her.)

GASTON. Madame!

ALICIA. Goodbye, Inez. You must come and call on us, dear boy. You're welcome any time. In my own home, I can chaperone Gilberte properly. *(She exits.)*

(MME. ALVAREZ returns to Left of GASTON, as GIGI speaks.)

GIGI. Grandma! You're not going to make me live with Aunt Alicia, are you? I don't want to leave here, Grandma!

MME. ALVAREZ. Now, now, you little idiot—we're going to cross that bridge when we come to it!

GASTON. *(Picking up his hat from dining-table)* Well, Mamita—I'm afraid I've got to run along.

(GIGI turns away to front.)

MME. ALVAREZ. If you must, Gaston.

GASTON. *(Looks at GIGI, puts hat back on table, and covering newspaper clipping, which ALICIA has left on the table. He goes to GIGI, at down Left)* Gigi—does it make you feel any better to know I'm sorry for everything I said today?

GIGI. *(Simply)* That's all right, Tonton. I can't be mad at you forever. *(GIGI does not look at him—after a pause, she offers him her hand.)*

(The clock strikes ONE.)

GASTON. *(Grasping her hand)* Good! Mamita! *(Crossing up to Right of MME. ALVAREZ)* Now that she looks like our own sweet little angel once again, why can't Gigi go with me?

GIGI. Go? Go where?

GASTON. To the Bois, for an ice.

GIGI. *(Turning to them)* Oh, Grandma, may I?

MME. ALVAREZ. No, Gilberte.

GIGI. But why not?

GASTON. She doesn't have to tell her Aunt about it, you know.

GIGI. *(Crossing up to MME. ALVAREZ)* Please!

MME. ALVAREZ. Not this time, dear. Run into the kitchen, and see if Sidonie has put the kettle on, will you?

GIGI. Oh, all right, Grandma. *(Exits into kitchen.)*

MME. ALVAREZ. I hate to seem difficult, Gaston—but you understand my position, don't you?

GASTON. Can't say that I do. It seems to me you're making an elephant out of a flea.

MME. ALVAREZ. But, my dear boy, I'm only acting as a mother would. I have a sacred trust, to guard Gigi like a tender flower.

GASTON. Well, I won't argue about it. Just go on protecting your brat.

(From the kitchen comes the SOUND of the tea-kettle crashing to the floor.)

MME. ALVAREZ. Oh, that wretched Sidonie! *(Crossing to kitchen)* What is it this time? *(She exits.)*

GIGI'S VOICE. Me, Grandma! I dropped the tea-kettle, that's all.

(GASTON picks up his hat, revealing the newspaper clipping; takes it and reads. From the kitchen we hear:)

MME. ALVAREZ. You didn't hurt yourself?

GIGI. No, Grandma—I guess I was a little bit nervous.

MME. ALVAREZ. Well, be careful now!

GIGI. I will!

(MME. ALVAREZ enters to Left of table, suddenly sees GASTON reading about LIANE.)

MME. ALVAREZ. *(Trying to seem casual)* Imagine the faker! Trying to commit suicide!

    (GASTON looks at her, replacing paper on table.)

Lucky escape you had from that one! *(WARN Curtain.)*

GASTON. Think so? Well, I've got to get along. *(Crossing up Right of table, to door.)*

MME. ALVAREZ. *(Following him)* I'll just fetch Gigi, to say goodbye.

GASTON. *(Quickly)* Don't bother; I'll see her some other time.

MME. ALVAREZ. Tomorrow, perhaps? *(Moving to Right side of front door.)*

GASTON. *(Going through door)* Perhaps. I'm afraid I'll be pretty busy the next few weeks. Goodbye! *(Exits and closes door.)*

(SIDONIE enters from kitchen, just in time to see GASTON leave. MME. ALVAREZ crosses down to above table. SIDONIE crosses to Left of MME. ALVAREZ.)

SIDONIE. This may not be my business, Madame—but I think you've gone one step too far with that young man.

MME. ALVAREZ. *(Shortly)* It's not your business—and nobody pays you to think! *(Takes clipping from table, starts to read.)*

SIDONIE. Very well, Madame, but what in the world could he be doing that would take him several weeks? *(Picks up half-empty champagne bottle.)*

MME. ALVAREZ. Shut up! And get along with your work!

SIDONIE. Better look out, Madame— If Monsieur Lachaille can leave you, *I* can!! *(Exits to kitchen, looking into bottle, hopefully.)*

(As LIGHTS dim, MME. ALVAREZ crumples clipping, crosses, sits Right of table, worried and upset.)

CURTAIN

ACT TWO

SCENE II

SCENE: *Alicia's boudoir. Same as Act One, Scene Two, except that the telephone stand is now at the Left end of the chaise-longue, replacing the small stand. Also, the chaise-longue has been moved to a 30-degree angle.*

The telephone receiver is off the hook.

After the Curtain has risen, ALICIA enters from Left, goes to front of chaise-longue, sits, and talks into the phone. She is wearing another elaborate negligee. GIGI enters, stands listening in door Right.

ALICIA. Hello, Inez—it's *you* again! I do wish you'd leave this affair to *me!* I'm telling you, you almost *lost* the man for good, so from now on, you'll just keep out of things, if you don't mind.—What if he didn't go back to Liane? He didn't go back to you, either—he came to *me.*

And what's more important, he's coming here this afternoon,—and I think he's going to make a proposition,—
for Gilberte, not *you*, dear! Yes, and I've spent the last
three hours working out a counter-proposition that will
be absolutely water-tight— But of course, Lachaille will
protect his own interests, down to the last penny. Don't
forget he has one of the best business brains in France—
No, please, Inez, don't come over here again! I hate to
sound inhospitable, but you've been running in here,
two and three times a day, and upsetting Gigi. She
appears to hanker for that run-down flat of yours, and
the perfume of stale cooking. If you have anything important to say, you have a telephone—*use* it!! *(Conscious of* GIGI's *presence, turns and sees her)* Ah,
Gilberte, my dear—how sweet you look! *(Into phone)*
Gilberte!—she's wearing my rose chiffon negligee—yes,
ravishing! Very well, dear, you may call up later. Goodbye! *(Hangs up. Takes magazine from lower end of chaise-
longue, casually thumbs through it.)*
    GIGI. *(Crossing to chair down Right)* What did
Grandma want, Aunty?
    ALICIA. The address of the doctor who looks after
Madame Dufour—for indigestion.
    GIGI. Grandma's indigestion?
    ALICIA. Gilberte—you were listening at the door!
        *(*GIGI *looks at her.)*
A person should never listen at doors, my dear. It's the
best way I know to hear incorrectly and misunderstand
things.
        *(*GIGI *sits on chair Right, leans on its back, facing
        audience.* ALICIA *puts down magazine, rises, crosses
        to Center.)*
Now, what can your dull old Aunty do to take that
gloom away?
    GIGI. I'm not gloomy, Aunt Alicia.
    ALICIA. Yes, you are, dear—and it's not very attrac-
tive. *(Taking a ring from her finger, crosses to* GIGI*)*
Here! How about wearing my ring for a while? *(Puts it
on* GIGI's *left hand.)*

GIGI. *(Politely)* It's very pretty.

ALICIA. It's much more than pretty, my dear child. That diamond has the shimmer of a pure white star.

GIGI. Jewels make you feel poetic, don't they, Aunt Alicia?

ALICIA. *(Crossing to Right end of chaise-longue)* Well, why not, dear?

GIGI. Oh, they're lovely, of course—but when I feel poetic, it's about—

ALICIA. *(Turning to her)* About what?

GIGI. *(Resuming her pose, staring into space)* Oh, about—flowers—or a view—or sometimes music—

ALICIA. *(Suddenly interested)* Gilberte! Could it be —oh no, it couldn't be that, at your age.

GIGI. *(Glancing at her)* What—at my age?

ALICIA. Could it be that you're—in love?

GIGI. Who with?

ALICIA. Your darling Tonton,—who else?

GIGI. Oh, I like Tonton very much, Aunty—of course.

ALICIA. But you're not in love with him?

GIGI. *(Looking into space)* No, Aunty.

ALICIA. Well, he's a very handsome man—that Lachaille. One only has to see his photos, taken at Trouville, in a bathing-suit.

GIGI. *(Rises, quickly)* Aunty—I'd like to have a headache powder. I've got a headache.

(KNOCK on door.)

ALICIA. Come in.

VICTOR. *(Enters)* Monsieur Lachaille is downstairs, Madame.

ALICIA. Ask him if he will see an infirm old lady in her boudoir, Victor.

VICTOR. Yes, Madame. *(He starts to go.)*

ALICIA. And Victor—will you bring a headache powder to Mademoiselle Gilberte in her room?

VICTOR. Yes, Madame. *(Exits.)*

ALICIA. *(Going to GIGI, putting her arm about her shoulders)* Come, dear, you must lie down and rest for a

while. This is all a part of growing-up, my little Gilberte.
You're beginning to know what it means to be a woman.

GIGI. I wish I never had to grow up, Aunt Alicia.
(Drops her head on ALICIA'S *shoulder.)*

ALICIA. There, there, my dear! *(Takes* GIGI's *Left
hand and looks at ring)* It has its recompenses—now
come along, lie down for a bit—you'll soon feel better,
etc., etc. *(Leading her off Left.)*

(VICTOR *enters Right, takes chair from down Right,
places it Center, facing front, as* GASTON *enters.)*

VICTOR. Please take a seat, Monsieur. Madame won't
keep you waiting, I'm sure.

GASTON. Thanks. *(Sits.)*

VICTOR. *(Glances at door Left, moves from behind
chair to Right of* GASTON, *leans toward him and speaks
in low tone)* She's got the strategy of twenty rattlesnakes
—so be on your guard, Monsieur.

GASTON. You needn't worry, Victor—I'll remember
what you told me—one can clip a sheep every year, but
you can only skin him once.

ALICIA. *(Enters from Left)* Gaston, my dear!

GASTON. *(Rises, kisses her hand)* Madame!

ALICIA. I do apologize for keeping you waiting, my
dear boy.

GASTON. Oh, you needn't, Madame. Victor and I have
been putting in our time to a very good advantage.

ALICIA. *(With a look at* VICTOR) Splendid!

VICTOR. *(Taking his cue from* ALICIA's *look)* Thank
you, Madame. *(Exits Right.)*

ALICIA. Dear Victor! In forty years, he's never failed
me once. Sit down, Gaston. *(She sits on chaise-longue.)*

GASTON. Thank you.

ALICIA. And now what is it? What's on your mind, my
dear boy?

GASTON. *(Moves above, and around chair, to Right
of it)* Well, Madame, the thing that's on my mind was
put there several days ago, by you yourself.

ALICIA. Oh?

GASTON. It's—it's about your little Gilberte, Madame.

ALICIA. Really?

GASTON. *(Sits)* You see, Madame, the day when you mentioned that Gigi was—well—when you spoke about some nice man who might—well—insure her future, it gave me a terrible shock.

ALICIA. That's quite understandable.

GASTON. And then it began to give me a terrible scare. I had nightmares all that night— I thought I was seeing Gigi at the Cafe de Paris, with Georges Feydeau, in a private room with him—and then, the next morning, I began to realize how right you were, in saying she's grown up. She *has* grown up, Madame—right under my very nose.

ALICIA. Yes, Gaston—everybody concerned has been aware of it except you.

GASTON. Well, I should have known it would happen some day, but in my mind she's always been so fresh—so —well, so like a tomboy. And now, suddenly, to see her in another light—it's—it's—bewildering!

ALICIA. Yes, Gaston. All this is a little vague, isn't it? What have you got in mind that's a bit more definite?

GASTON. *(Earnestly)* Well—first of all, I'd like to assure you, Madame, that if I may have the privilage of —well—that she'll be taken care of as—as—

ALICIA. *(Helping him out)* As no other mistress has ever been taken care of?

GASTON. That's right, Madame. That's just what I meant to say. You see, my feelings for Gigi are—well, they're rather mixed, They're—

ALICIA. I know you'll pardon me for interrupting, Gaston, but as Gilberte's silly old aunt, who knows nothing about facts or figures, you're making the vague sort of statements that men always make. Suppose we get down to essentials?

GASTON. Oh, I don't wish to evade the essentials, Madame. I want to guarantee Gigi against every future worry—even against myself. In many ways, I'll be almost like—like a brother to her—or like a—

ALICIA. Yes, yes, Gaston—but now we're being vague again.

GASTON. *(Hopelessly)* Then what do *you* suggest, Madame?

ALICIA. *(Really ready with her proposal)* Well, the child will have to have a roof over her head—

GASTON. But certainly—

ALICIA. I propose a house on the Avenue de Bois—not enormous, but suitable—I'll find one for you.

GASTON. Why—thanks.

ALICIA. Then, seeing that Gilberte is completely inexperienced, she must have a competent staff. I suggest a first-rate major-domo.

GASTON. *(Agreeing)* Of course. And perhaps a maid, who will be old enough to mother her a little.

ALICIA. *A* maid, Gaston?

GASTON. Well, she'll need a maid, won't she, Madame?

ALICIA. In that house?—she'll need at least three!

GASTON. Oh!

ALICIA. Now, what about a motor-car?

GASTON. But I have two already, Madame!

ALICIA. Yes, yes, that might work out for the first year. But she'll be needing one of her own eventually, and now is the time to provide it.

GASTON. I see.

ALICIA. And while we're on the subject, Gaston,—I hate to be gloomy, but the pace at which you drive those cars of yours—well—something could happen to you at any time.

GASTON. Oh now, really, Madame!—

ALICIA. In case it *did*, what provision would you have made for Gilberte?

GASTON. But the house would be in her name, and—

ALICIA. A house in Paris? Suppose the Prussians traipsed in here—as they did in 1870?

GASTON. Well, as far as that goes, Madame—the world could come to an end!

ALICIA. That's a very wise observation. So, what about that little retreat of yours in the country?

GASTON. You mean Bon Abri?

ALICIA. Yes—Bon Abri. A sanctuary, to which Gilberte could retire at her time of mourning. How many acres does that property have?

GASTON. Just a moment, Madame—you're beginning to confuse me! The end of the world,—The Franco-Prussian War—an automobile accident—and the acreage at Bon Abri!—I'm way beyond depth!

ALICIA. Well, since we're rapidly getting nowhere, I have a good idea: why not meet me tomorrow some time at the office of my lawyer?

GASTON. I have an even better idea than *that*, Madame. Why don't you and your lawyer meet *me* in the office of *my* lawyer?

ALICIA. Your lawyer? You mean, Senator Flandin?

GASTON. Have you something against Flandin?

ALICIA. The cleverest lawyer in France? How could I?

GASTON. Shall we say ten o'clock tomorrow morning?

(There is a KNOCK at the door Right.)

ALICIA. Very well, dear boy, at ten tomorrow— Come in.

VICTOR. *(Enters)* Forgive me, Madame— *(Crossing to above chaise-longue)* —but Mademoiselle Gilberte asked me to bring you this. *(He hands ALICIA the diamond ring, with a piece of note-paper rolled up in it)* She said it was very urgent.

ALICIA. *(Opening note)* Where is Mademoiselle?

VICTOR. She's gone, Madame.

ALICIA. Gone? Gone where?

VICTOR. She said she was returning to her own home, Madame.

ALICIA. I see. Very well, Victor.

(VICTOR exits Right.)

GASTON. Has anything happened with Gigi?

ALICIA. No, no—just some of her usual childishness. *(She rises; suddenly takes refuge in becoming feeble.*

GASTON *also rises.)* And now, if you will excuse me, Gaston. One of my sudden headaches. Nerves, I suppose. I'm so unused to these horrid business matters.

GASTON. I'll run along, then—and I'll order the Senator to get in touch with your lawyer at once.

ALICIA. *(Quickly)* I'm afraid we'll have to drop things for the moment.   *(WARN Curtain.)*

GASTON. *(Two steps toward her)* What's the matter, Madame? Is there anything in that note of Gigi's that—

ALICIA. *(Stopping him)* No, of course not. Some silly notion that means nothing. I can always handle Gilberte. But you'll just have to give me a little more time, that's all.

GASTON. But, Madame—

ALICIA. *(Sinking to chaise-longue)* I really do feel rather ill, my dear boy. Do you mind? *(Extending her hand.)*

GASTON. *(Bowing, kissing her hand)* Of course not, Madame. *(Crosses to door Right, turns, bows)* Goodbye, —Madame.

ALICIA. *(About to spring into action, quickly strikes pose of fatigue, as* GASTON *turns for his final goodbye. After his exit, she rises, crosses above chaise-longue, to telephone. Pulls bell-pull on her way. Into phone)* Hello, Inez! I'm calling up to warn you that—hello, hello?— Give me number five hundred and eighty-one. I want five hundred and eighty-one!—Busy? What do you mean, busy?—Well, cut in on the line!—Oh very well, obey your stupid rules.—But tell me what she's saying!— Look here, young woman, this machine was invented to simplify life, not to complicate it.—Come over at once and take the damn thing away!!—Oh, you little bitch! *(Slams receiver down.)*

VICTOR. *(Has entered to hear* ALICIA's *last lines)* Did you say something, Madame?

ALICIA. Victor, I want the carriage at once! *(Crosses to door Left.)*

VICTOR. I told it to stand by. I thought Madame would be going to Madame Alvarez.

ALICIA. Why did you think that?

VICTOR. *(A step toward her)* I smelled trouble in the air, Madame.

ALICIA. Trouble, you idiot—it's disaster! *(She exits Right.)*

(VICTOR, emitting a comic sound of apprehension, exits, as LIGHTS DIM, and—)

THE CURTAIN FALLS

ACT TWO

Scene III

SCENE: *In Madame Alvarez' living-room. Later the same day.*

GIGI is at the telephone. She has draped her navy-blue coat over her head, so as to prevent the sound of her voice from being heard by MME. ALVAREZ, who is in the kitchen.

The scene is the same, except that the pouffe at Center has been moved to front of dining-table.

GIGI. Hello?—Hello! Is this the Jockey Club?—I'd like to speak to Monsieur Gaston Lachaille, please—Monsieur Gaston Lachaille! *(Continuing her heavy whisper)* Hello—oh. Well, as soon as he comes in, will you please say that Mademoiselle Gilberte Alvarez—
(One ring of DOORBELL.)
would like to see him at her home.—Yes, at her own home. Thank you, goodbye.

(Five rings of DOORBELL. GIGI hangs up the receiver, and runs quickly into the bedroom.)

MME. ALVAREZ. *(Entering from kitchen, to front door)* I'm coming—I'm coming! *(Opens door)* Alicia! For heaven's sake, what's the matter?

ALICIA. *(Enters in a state of furious excitement, crosses down to Right Center)* Where's that grandchild of yours?

MME. ALVAREZ. *(Moving down to Left Center)* Gigi?

ALICIA. What other grandchild have you?

MME. ALVAREZ. Alicia! Isn't she with *you?*

ALICIA. *No!* Lachaille was all ready to meet my lawyer, when she ruined everything by disappearing. Isn't she here?

MME. ALVAREZ. Why no! I don't think so! I've been cleaning the stove. *(She goes to door Left and calls)* Gigi! Gigi!

GIGI'S VOICE. Yes, Grandma?

MME. ALVAREZ. Thank God! *(Sinks into sofa.)*

GIGI'S VOICE. Do you want me, Grandma?

MME. ALVAREZ. Yes, darling. Your Aunt's here.

ALICIA. *(To Center)* Come in here, Gilberte! Immediately!

GIGI'S VOICE. I'm not ready!

ALICIA. Well, hurry up then!

MME. ALVAREZ. The poor little rabbit!

ALICIA. The poor little rabbit! Would you like to hear an ultimatum that has just been issued to me by your poor little rabbit?

MME. ALVAREZ. Ultimatum, Alicia?

ALICIA. An ultimatum. Before she traipsed out of my house just now, she sent me a note to say that the only way she might possibly consider Gaston, would be to talk things over with him herself—alone.

MME. ALVAREZ. Well, after all, the matter concerns nobody but Gigi.

ALICIA. Do you mean that I—Alicia de St. Ephlam, should turn this extremely delicate and complicated affair over to a silly child who's incapable of realizing her luck? *(Takes a few steps to down Right.)*

MME. ALVAREZ. Alicia—don't you think we've been rushing Gigi a little bit? I'm afraid she hasn't yet reached the point of wanting Gaston.

ALICIA. *(Crossing to Center)* That's understandable at the moment. She's too used to him, as some sort of a sexless uncle, or cousin, or other. Her imagination must be aroused. She must be talked to.

MME. ALVAREZ. I have talked to her.

ALICIA. And what sort of argument did *you* use on the young lady?

MME. ALVAREZ. I told her how reliable Gaston is— what a substantial character he has.

ALICIA. And you never took the trouble to mention love? You didn't talk to her about long voyages and moonlight? You never mentioned that on the other side of the world, there are humming birds in the flowers, and how delicate it is to make love in the moonlight, beside marble fountains?

MME. ALVAREZ. How could I? The farthest I've ever been is Strasburg!

ALICIA. You're not capable of inventing anything? *(Crosses Right.)*

MME. ALVAREZ. No, Alicia.

ALICIA. Good God!

GIGI. *(Enters from bedroom)* What do you want with me, Aunt Alicia?

ALICIA. Come here! I want an explanation!!

MME. ALVAREZ. *(As GIGI crosses slowly to Center)* Please don't scold the child, Alicia! Can't you see she's nervous! *(To GIGI)* Don't you worry about anything, my darling. Nobody's going to torment you about Tonton!

(GIGI looks over her shoulder at MME. ALVAREZ.)

ALICIA. *(Crossing to Center, to Right of GIGI—trying more gentle tactics)* No, of course not! But at the same time, I do wish you'd use a little common-sense. Some women don't fall in love before thirty—or even later. And it really might have been a pity for you to have to have started out your career with a grand passion. Fascinating as it would be to go to the end of the world with a man who knows everything there is to know about life. To lose one's self in the arms of a divine creature like Gaston Lachaille.—To listen to love songs under a sky of eternal springtime!—

(GIGI *slowly looks at* ALICIA.)
Of course, if that doesn't appeal to you, there's nothing more to be said!*(Crossing to down Right.)*

GIGI. There's something more than that I can say, Aunty. I can say that when the "eternal Springtime" is over, Monsieur Lachaille may go off with another woman —perhaps the woman, even I, may run away from Monsieur Lachaille, and Monsieur Lachaille will tell the story to everyone at the Jockey Club. And the woman, who could still be I, might have nothing to do but go straight into the bed of some other man!

ALICIA. Inez! She's speaking the language of the gutter!

GIGI. I'm sorry, Aunty. But I just don't care for that way of living. I'm not that changeable.

ALICIA. Very well, then, if you want to end up working at a dressmaking shop, or in the chorus of the Opera Comique—go ahead and do it! *(Sits in armchair Right.)*

GIGI. *(Few steps to* ALICIA) You think you know so much, Aunt Alicia! You think you've done so brilliantly in life! Well, do you know what *I* think? I think that you're a failure!!

ALICIA. What?

GIGI. What have you got out of that elegant career of yours, except a houseful of silly knick-knacks? Why, you're so bored, you have to trump up headaches, just to keep yourself company!

ALICIA. That will do, Gilberte!

MME. ALVAREZ. Don't scold her, Alicia! I've never believed much in those headaches myself!

GIGI. *(Quickly interrupting—crosses few steps to* MME. ALVAREZ) And *you* Grandma! You've sided with her about Tonton—you *know* you have!

MME. ALVAREZ. I only wanted to save you from poverty, my child.

GIGI. But *why?* We've always been poor, you and Maman and I—and has it been so bad? Why, Tonton himself has to come here for a decent cup of camomile! Both of you!—with your plans and schemes, and your advice—maybe I can work some way out myself, that will be better!

ALICIA. If you have a plan for the future, my dear, I should be most interested to hear it!

GIGI. Oh, it isn't that I *know* what it will be—I just can't think too hard about it—not yet! I'm awfully fond of Tonton. I enjoy our games of piquet. *(Looks toward* ALICIA*) Not* on account of his money, but because he's fun. I'd like to spend my life with him. It would be very pleasant—but—

(Three rings of DOORBELL.)

MME. ALVAREZ. *(Gives a start. Rises)* Gaston!

ALICIA. *(Rises)* She mustn't see him while she's in this state!

MME. ALVAREZ. Go to your room, Gilberte!

GIGI. *(With authority)* No, Grandma! I've got to know what Tonton has to say. I've got to see him.
    (Three rings of DOORBELL.)
(To ALICIA*)* Please, Aunty!

ALICIA. Very well, Gilberte. *(Crossing to bedroom door Left)* But just remember in the future that this was your own doing. *(Exits.)*

GIGI. *(To* MME. ALVAREZ*)* Go along, Grandma!
    *(*MME. ALVAREZ *starts to door—stops, looks back to* GIGI.*)*
Please?

MME. ALVAREZ. All right, dear. *(Exits to bedroom.)*

(Three rings of DOORBELL. GIGI *runs to mirror, Right, fixes her hair, rushes up Right of table to front door. Pauses to compose herself, then opens the door, and* GASTON *steps inside. They face each other for a moment in silence.)*

GIGI. Good day, Tonton.

GASON. You didn't want to open the door for me, you bad girl.

GIGI. I'm sorry, Tonton, but I was asleep.

(They stare at each other for a moment, then suddenly
BOTH *reach to close door.* GIGI'S *head bumps*
against GASTON'S *shoulder.)*

GASTON. Oh, I'm sorry. *(He closes the door.)*
GIGI. Won't you come in?
GASTON. Thanks.

(GIGI *walks down Right of table*—GASTON *Left of it.*
They pause.)

GIGI. So you got my message at the Club, did you?
GASTON. Why no—I haven't been there.
GIGI. Then why did you come here?
GASTON. I wanted to make sure you got home safely
from your Aunt's, that's all.
GIGI. Oh! *(Glances at* GASTON, *trying to make con-*
versation) Well, Tonton,—you look very elegant in your
swallow-tail.
GASTON. It's a cutaway, stupid.
GIGI. Of course it is. Where are my brains? Will you
sit down?

(GASTON *takes chair from Left of dining-table, places it*
Left Center as GIGI *takes chair from Right of table,*
and places it Right Center.)

GASTON. Yes. *(Sits, but rises quickly, until* GIGI *has*
seated herself. He sits again) Sorry! *(Slight pause)*
Gigi— *(Gives a slight tug at his chair towards her)*
—there's something I'd like to ask you. Tell me something. Did you know what I went to see your Aunt Alicia
about today?
GIGI. *(Half turned toward him)* I understand you told
Aunt Alicia that you would be willing to—
GASTON. *(Interrupting her)* Please! I know what I said
to your Aunt. It isn't necessary for you to repeat it.

(Again moves his chair a few inches toward hers) Just
tell me what it is you don't want. And then tell me what
it is you *do* want. I'll give it to you if I can.

GIGI. Really?

GASTON. I'll try.

GIGI. Well, you told Aunty that you wished to give
me a future.

GASTON. A very good one, Gigi.

GIGI. It would be a good one, if I wanted it, Tonton.
But the way you want things—well,—it seems I'm to
leave here, and go away with you and sleep in your bed.

GASTON. *(Avoiding her gaze)* Don't, Gigi—please.

GIGI. But why should I be ashamed to say things to
you, that you weren't ashamed to say to Aunt Alicia?
I know very well that if you gave me a future, Tonton,
I'll have my picture in the papers,—I'll go to the Flower
Festival at Nice, and to the races at Trouville. But every
time we have a quarrel, *Gil Blas* will tell all about it,
and when you leave me for good, as you did when you
had enough of Gaby Fougere—

GASTON. How did you know about that? *(Again moving his chair toward her)* Have they told you these
things?

GIGI. Nobody had to tell me. I just know what everybody else in the world knows. I know that you're a very
fashionable man. I know that Maryse Chuquet stole some
letters from you, and that you had to bring suit against
her. I know that the Countess Pariewsky was upset because you wouldn't marry a divorced woman, and that
she shot at you with a revolver.

GASTON. *(Moves his chair. He is now very close to her)*
But all those things had nothing to do with *you*, Gigi.
That's all finished. It's in the past. *(Takes her hands.)*

GIGI. That's true, Tonton—up to the point when it
begins again. It isn't your fault that you're fashionable.
But you see, I just haven't any desire to be fashionable
myself. *(Draws her hands away from his)* So things like
that don't tempt me. *(Rises)* You see, that's the way it

is. *(Steps down Right, turns away from him)* That's just how it happens to be.

GASTON. *(Rises)* Gigi—I'd like to be sure you're not simply trying to hide the fact that I'm not pleasing to you. If I'm not, it's better that I know about it right away.

GIGI. *(Looks at him)* Why no, Tonton, I'm very happy when I see you. *(Going to him)* The proof is, that I'm going to propose something myself. You may come here as usual, only more often. No one will see anything wrong with it, because you're a friend of the family. You can bring me licorice and champagne for my birthday, and on Sunday, we'll play a simply monstrous game of piquet. Well—isn't that a much better way to do things, than to have the newspapers print that I'm sleeping with you, so that everyone in Paris knows about it?

GASTON. But—there's one thing, Gigi, you seem to have overlooked. And that is that—that I'm in love with you.

GIGI. *(Utterly dazed)* You're in love with me? But you never told me that before!

GASTON. I'm telling you now.

GIGI. *(Horror-stricken, pushes her chair upstage, and moves closer to GASTON)* What kind of a horrible man are you, anyway?

GASTON. Gigi!

GIGI. You're in love with me! And you want to drag me into a life that can only bring me suffering? Where everybody talks viciously about everybody else—where the newspapers write nasty stories—? You're in love with me! But it doesn't stop you for a moment from wanting to drag me into something that's bound to end up with a separation—with quarrels—with revolvers—with laudanum? With another woman for you and another man for me? And then another, and another, and another! *(Breaks into a sob, and covers her face with her hands.)*

GASTON. But, Gigi—listen to me—

GIGI. *(Bursting in)* Go away! I never want to see you again. I'd never have believed it of you—you couldn't be in love with anyone— Get out of here!! *(Shrieks)* Get out— Get out!!!

(During the above, MME. ALVAREZ enters from bedroom, followed by ALICIA.)

MME. ALVAREZ. What is it, child? What has happened?

ALICIA. What was she screaming about?

GASTON. *(Two steps to Center, facing MME. ALVAREZ)* Your niece has just ordered me to leave the house! She just informed me she doesn't want me!

ALICIA. Gilberte!

MME. ALVAREZ. Gigi!

GASTON. She doesn't want me! *(Crossing up to foyer. ALICIA follows up to Left of him, and MME. ALVAREZ up to Right of him)* It's the first time it's ever been said to my face. I'm not likely to misunderstand!

ALICIA. I don't know what to say about this, Gaston.

GASTON. It's all right—think no more about it!

ALICIA. That's generous of you, dear boy— perhaps when the child—

GASTON. Please! Don't bother her about me any more! I'm just as fed up with the whole thing as *she* is! *(Exits, slamming door.)*

(Together)

MME. ALVAREZ. *(Crossing down, Right of table, to GIGI, who has crossed Right to mantel—leans on it, sobbing)* You unhappy child—what have you done to us?

GIGI. Oh, let me alone, Grandma—please!

ALICIA. *(Who has crossed down, Left of table, to Center)* Stop that snivelling at once, and tell us what happened?

GIGI. *(Speaking through her sobs)* He said he was in love with me.

(MME. ALVAREZ and ALICIA exchange glances.)

ALICIA. I don't believe I heard you correctly.

GIGI. *(Over her shoulder)* Tonton said he was in love with me.

MME. ALVAREZ. Well, you poor little ninny, what did you expect?

ALICIA. Do you think a man takes a mistress because she nauseates him?

GIGI. No, Aunty—I understand. But it wasn't only that. He couldn't even tell me that he wanted to go to bed with me.—He couldn't say the words—they were so dreadful. So I ordered him out of here, and never come near me again. *(Buries her head in her arms.)*

ALICIA. Well, that's the end!

MME. ALVAREZ. She's exactly like her mother! I don't know what I've done, to deserve such worthless children!

GIGI. I'm sorry, Grandma.

ALICIA. She brings the ceiling down on our heads, and she says she's sorry!

(Three rings of DOORBELL.)

Who is that?

MME. ALVAREZ. It can't be Gaston! If there's one thing Gaston has, it's pride.

(Turns to go to door. GIGI stops her.)

GIGI. Grandma, wait! If it *is* Tonton, I can't see him again! *(Runs to bedroom door.)*

MME. ALVAREZ. Gigi—stay where you are!

GIGI. *(In doorway)* Please, Grandma—I can't stand any more of this—ever!

ALICIA. Leave the room, if you wish, Gilberte!

(GIGI exits.)

MME. ALVAREZ But, Alicia—

ALICIA. Let the child go! Can't you see she's got a method in her madness?

MME. ALVAREZ. Method? What method?

(Three rings of DOORBELL.)

ALICIA. He's come back, hasn't he?

(The light beginning to dawn, MME. ALVAREZ rushes up to door, to admit GASTON. GASTON enters hurriedly, to Center, addressing ALICIA. He carries a fresh box of licorice.)

GASTON. I don't want to intrude, but there's no reason Gigi shouldn't have the licorice I brought here. I left it in my car.

MME. ALVAREZ. *(Quickly follows GASTON, down to front of sofa)* Thanks, Gaston—that's generous of you.

GASTON. *(Turns to MME. ALVAREZ)* Well, you can hardly call it generous—it only cost— *(He hurls the box of licorice to the floor, drops to one knee, and appeals to MME. ALVAREZ)* Mamita! Will you grant me the honor, the favor, the infinite joy of Gigi's hand?

MME. ALVAREZ. *(Bewildered)* Gigi's—hand?

ALICIA. *(A few steps to Right of GASTON)* Gaston, we're being vague again.

GASTON. *(Rises—addresses ALICIA)* I am asking for Gigi's hand in marriage!

MME. ALVAREZ. *(Stunned, sits on sofa)* Alicia!

ALICIA. Well, it's rather unconventional, dear boy— *(Starting to door Left in a gay mood)* Let's see what Gilberte has to say about it. *(Opens door and calls off)* Gilberte!!

GIGI. *(Enters)* Has he gone, Aunty?

MME. ALVAREZ. Gigi, Monsieur Lachaille has just made a proposal for your hand in marriage.

GASTON. *(At Center)* I want you to be my wife, Gigi.
    (GIGI drops her head, starts to cry.)
Gigi! What is it? You're crying! What is it, Gigi?

GIGI. I'm ashamed.

GASTON. Ashamed?

ALICIA. *(A step to GIGI)* Ashamed of what, Child?

GIGI. I've been acting like all those bad women Tonton's had—upsetting you—making you unhappy— Only I'm not like them, really, because I love you.

GASTON. Gigi!

GIGI. I love you, Tonton. *(Runs to him at Center, throwing her arms about him, sobs on his shoulder)* I love you! *(Pause)* You don't have to marry me.

(MME. ALVAREZ rises; ALICIA a few steps in, greatly alarmed.)

ALICIA. Gilberte!

GIGI. Do anything you want with me. Take me away, right now, if you like.

MME. ALVAREZ. Gigi—that's enough, now! *(Appeals to ALICIA.)*

GASTON. It's all right, Mamita. *(Holding GIGI in his arms)* Don't you see, Gigi, this is the only way I could have taken you. I just didn't understand it before—that's all.

(They kiss. ANDREE enters from door.)

ANDREE. Why, Gigi! Gigi, dear. *(Crosses down, Right of table to Right of GASTON)* Gaston, what is it?

MME. ALVAREZ. *(From front of sofa)* Our little Gigi has consented to become Madame Lachaille!

ANDREE. —Madame—Lachaille—?

(GIGI and GASTON turn to ANDREE.)

(WARN Curtain.)

GIGI. Tonton and I, Maman. We're going to be married.

ANDREE. Married?— *(Bursts into tears, covering her face with her hands)* Gigi! Ohhhh! Oh, Gigi!

GIGI. *(Rushes to Right of ANDREE, holds her in her arms)* Maman! Don't cry, Maman!

(ANDREE cries all the harder.)

Tonton! *Do* something!!

GASTON. *(Looking toward MME. ALVAREZ and ALICIA)* Perhaps a drink would help her!

MME. ALVAREZ. *(Quickly moving to Center, eager to put a stop to this suggestion)* No!

ALICIA. *(Crossing in a few steps)* Andree! Compose yourself!

GASTON. *(Turning to* ANDREE*)* Listen, Andree, we're happy! We want you to help us celebrate!

(More loud crying from ANDREE.*)*

GIGI. Yes—please, Maman!

MME. ALVAREZ. *(Hoping to soothe her)* How'd you like to sing something?

ANDREE. *(Not quite sure she heard correctly)* Huh?

GASTON. Would you like to sing something?

*(*ANDREE'S *tears slowly vanish, as* GASTON *and* GIGI *move her toward piano. As they reach Center,* ANDREE *faces* ALICIA, *who is front of sofa.)*

ANDREE. May I?

ALICIA. *(Sinking into sofa)* If you must.

*(*ANDREE *crosses above sofa to piano stool, breathless with anticipation.* MME. ALVAREZ *crosses to upstage end of sofa.* GIGI *to chair Center.* GASTON *crosses to chair Right of* GIGI.*)*

ANDREE. *(At piano, turns to* OTHERS*)* Anything special?

MME. ALVAREZ. *(Grimly making the supreme sacrifice)* The Bell Song!

*(*ANDREE *quickly sits at the piano, plays introductory chords, as the* OTHERS *solemnly sit and just* WAIT. ANDREE *sings the opening phrase—with her usual off-key touch. The* OTHERS, *as one, cringe.* ANDREE *continues the Bell Song—and the Curtain falls.)*

FIRST CALL: *To the music of "Pot-pourri de Steps,"*

SIDONIE *enters from down Right to Center.* VICTOR *enters from down Left to Center. They meet, bow to each other, to the audience, and, to the rhythm of the music, exit Left.*

ANDREE *enters from down Right to the rhythm of the music, singing as she goes, exits Left.*

ALICIA *enters from down Right.* MME. ALVAREZ *from down Left. Walking in rhythm, they meet Center, bow to each other and to the audience.* MME. ALVAREZ *strikes typical Spanish pose, as* ALICIA *curtseys. They exit gayly, Left.*

GIGI *enters down Right,* GASTON *down Left. They meet Center. Bow to each other and to the audience, and as they turn again to each other, they embrace and kiss, and exit in opposite directions.*

CURTAIN

GIGI

PROPERTY PLOT

ACT ONE

Scene I

Alvarez living room.

Piano Left
Sofa Left
Small table front of sofa
Pouffe Center
Armchair Right by fireplace
Chair down Right
Small stove front of fireplace
Dining table up Center
Straight chairs Right and Left of table
Daybed under window up Right
Sideboard up stage Right Center
Wall hat rack in upstage alcove
Small wall mirror upstage
Picture of Gigi on Left wall
Picture of Andree on Left wall
Draperies at arch Center
Clock on mantel
China box with licorice on down stage end mantel
Playing cards on upstage end of mantel
Velvet cover on table
   On Sideboard
Curling irons (2) ⎤
Matches (large)   ⎟
Alcohol stove   ⎬   All on small tray.
Curl papers   ⎟
Comb   ⎦

Silver polish and dobber
Polish rag
Table silver (knives, forks and spoons)
Dining cloth
Ladies small purse with French coins on mantel
Old daily (French) paper on table front of sofa
 Off stage (outside front door)
String shopping bag filled with provisions (Alvarez)
Copy of "Gil Blas" (French paper)
Copy of "Comoedia" (French magazine)
 Off in kitchen (on tray)
Two cups and saucers, two spoons
Tea leaves in cups, sugar and spoon on each saucer
Hot water kettle with enough water to fill cups
Bunch of small carrots (with green tops) wrapped in
 single piece of newspaper
Paring knife
 Effects
Door bell
Door chimes
Phone bell

No prop strike

ACT ONE

Scene II

Alicia's house

Small desk down Left
Chair by desk
Phone on table above chaise
Note paper and pen on table
Small ornament box (with ring in it) on table
Bell rope on wall Left
Small foot stool under chaise
Gold chair Right
Rug draperies, etc.
Small stand at Left end of chaise

Off Right
Silver tray with glass of water and pill box
Off Left
Large jewel box with jewels (see S.M.)
Strike
End table
Re-set furniture for Act II/2 marks

ACT ONE

Scene III

Alvarez living room

Darning basket with all contents including large egg
Ladies' stockings on settee
Gold jeweled cigarette case (for Gaston) front
French newspaper on settee table
Dishes and other tableware on sideboard for table
setting

ACT TWO

Scene I

Alvarez living room

Add wall telephone
Reset Center table as opening of Act One
Strike cups of tea, darning basket, cards, carrots, knife,
etc.
Check sideboard setup as it was in Act One
Off stage by front door
Suitcase of champagne (4 quarts 2 pints in straw covers)
Leather music roll with fan inside, also school papers
Operette music score (off Left)
Champagne popper (in kitchen)
String bag with parcels off by front door, as in Act One
Water tumbler with champagne in it off in kitchen

Glass crash (a plate being dropped) in kitchen
Pieces of broken plate off in kitchen
Wrapped bouquet of flowers off by front door
Rubber ball on elastic off by front door
Tray with closed bottle of champagne (qt.)
Three champagne glasses also on tray off in kitchen
Folded section of French paper to fit into Alicia's bag
  Off Left
Gigi's school props: pencils, ink, and pen ruler, small
    books, cigarette case (gold one used in Act One)

ACT TWO

SCENE II

Alicia's

Ring in ornament box
Move foot stool to mark
  Off Right
Empty string bag (Alvarez)
Ring (get from Gigi) with piece of note paper (writing
    on it); paper is rolled and stuck through ring:
    Victor

ACT TWO

SCENE III

Living room

Strike chair down Right
Replace with armchair from front of fireplace
Move pouffe from stage Center to front of dining table
Box of licorice off by front door (Gaston)
Stove cleaning rag off in kitchen

GIGI

COSTUME PLOT

(Period, 1900—Paris, France)

Act One, Scene I

GIGI:

Sailor dress—black cotton stockings, black button shoes.
White lace petticoat and drawers.
Dark coat (navy blue) with small shoulder·cape.
Navy blue brim hat, with ribbon streamers.
Flat black bow on hair.

MME. ALVAREZ:

Black dress with beaded lace yoke.
Black shoes.
Tan coat with shoulder cape.
Black hat with small black ostrich plumes.
Black ostrich boa.
(Same throughout the play.)

ANDREE:

Faded pink negligee, crepe and lace.
White bloomers, corset cover, grey corset.
White petticoat with lace ruffles.
Red velvet skirt and blouse to match.
Red velvet hat, with red ostrich plumes.
Beaded bag and gloves. Black slippers.

GASTON:

Black and white check trousers.
Black frock coat. Tan top-coat. Silk hat.
Yellow gloves. Black cane. Wing collar, red tie.
Black button shoes.

Act One, Scene II

GIGI:
Same as Act One, Scene I.
VICTOR:
Butler's costume. Black trousers.
Yellow and white striped vest, brass buttons.
Black dress-coat. Wing collar, black bow-tie.
Black congress shoes.
ALICIA:
Rose pink pleated negligee, trimmed with cream lace.
Satin slippers to match. Cream lace fichu on head.
Jewelry.

Act One, Scene III

GIGI:
Same as previous scenes.
GASTON:
Same.
ANDREE:
Same, as in exit of Scene I.

Act Two, Scene I

GIGI:
Same, without cape.
Changes to yellow and white ruffled dress of period, with
gold buckle. Leg-of-mutton sleeves and bow-sash.
Black patent leather slippers. Flat blue bow on hair.
ANDREE:
Repeat negligee over petticoat.
ALICIA:
Black ruffled faille dress.
Short cape with cut-out velvet design over yellow silk.
Small black bonnet. Black muff, with small bunch of
yellow flowers on it.
Black gloves and shoes. Jewelled brooch at throat.
SIDONIE:
Black dress. Worn blue apron.

Short black crocheted shawl. Black shoes.
Change during scene to white apron, and removing shawl.
GASTON:
Tan plaid suit. Tan button boots.
Straw hat. Light stick (cane).
VICTOR:
Black topcoat, fly-buttoned. Black derby hat.
Grey muffler.

Act Two, Scene II

GIGI:
Duplicate of Alicia's negligee, Act One, Scene II.
Pink mules.
ALICIA:
Orchid chiffon negligee, under bottle-green robe with train.
Black lace fichu on head, caught with rhinestones.
Black satin slippers.
GASTON:
Morning trousers. Black cutaway coat. Brown tie.
Black patent leather shoes. Dark red carnation.
VICTOR:
Same as in Act One, Scene II.

Act Two, Scene III

GIGI:
Same as Act One.
ALICIA:
Repeat black dress. Ermine cape.
Small ermine hat, with Bird-of-Paradise feather.
Ermine muff. Black gloves. Bunch of violets at neck.
GASTON:
Same.
ANDREE:
Dark green wool skirt. White blouse.
Short black wool coat, with heavy lace collar.
Hat with pink rose trimming. Black slippers.
Bag and gloves as in Act Two, Scene I.

GIGI

LIGHTING

Act One, Scene I

Daytime.
General lighting. Bright sunlight through window.
Fireplace on.
Wizards in the exits.
Scene "fades in" through scrim at opening.
Fast dim, end of scene.

Scene II

Daytime "Fades in" through scrim.
Bright white light through window.
General lighting, with accent on chaise longue Left.
Slow dim—-end of scene.

Scene III

Evening. Fade in through scrim.
Hanging lamp and lamp on mantel added.
Window, low at opening, fades to out on cue.
No fade at end of scene.

ACT TWO

Scene I

Daytime. Open full up.
Fireplace off.
Fast dim—end of scene.

Scene II

Daytime. Fade in through scrim.
Set-up: same as Act One, Scene II.
Fast dim—end of scene.

Scene III

Fade in to Act One, Scene I, set-up.

GIGI

MUSIC PLOT

Scrim drops are used before the following scenes:
Act One, Scenes I, II, and III.
Act Two, Scenes II and III.
Recorded music used for scrims and scene-changes, as follows:
Act One:
Opening: "Potpourri de Valses"—Columbia DF 3365.
End of Scene I: "Promenade Tyrolienne"—Columbia DCF 44.
End of Scene II: "Potpourri de Valsees"—Columbia DF 3366.
Act Two:
End of Scene I: "Fascination"—Odeon 282480.
End of Scene II: "La Valse Brune"—Odeon 250218.
End of Scene III: "Potpourri de Steps"—Columbia DF 3365.
(French recordings.)

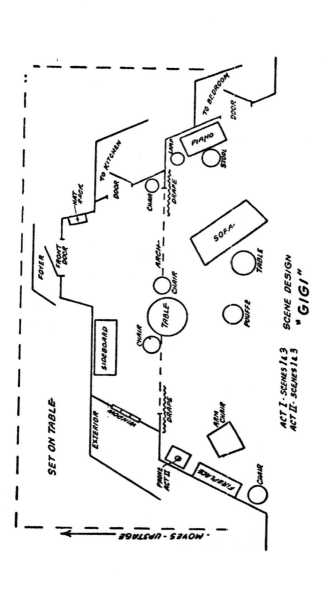

SET ON TABLE

'MOVES - UPSTAGE

EXTERIOR

FOYER

FRONT DOOR

HAT RACK

TO KITCHEN

DOOR

WINDOW

SIDEBOARD

WINDOW DRAPE

PHONE ACT II

FIREPLACE

ARM CHAIR

CHAIR

CHAIR

TABLE

ARCH

CHAIR

PUUFFE

TABLE

SOFA

DRAPE

CHAIR

LAMP

PIANO

STOOL

TO BEDROOM

DOOR

SCENE DESIGN
"GIGI"

ACT I - SCENES 1 & 3
ACT II - SCENES 1 & 3

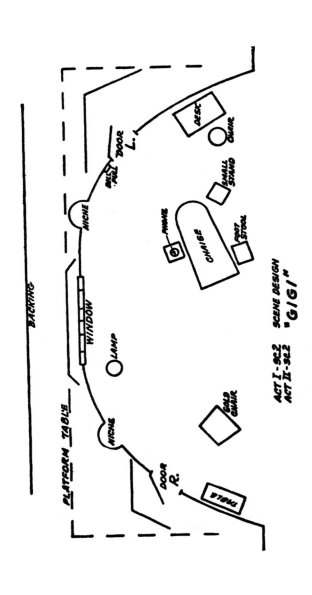

BACKING

PLATFORM TABLE

NICHE

WINDOW

LAMP

NICHE

DOOR R.

TABLE

OLD CHAIR

PHONE

CHAISE

FOOT STOOL

SMALL STAND

DESK

CHAIR

BELL PULL DOOR L.

ACT I - SC.2   SCENE DESIGN
ACT II - SC.2   "GIGI"

CPSIA information can be obtained at www.ICGtesting.com
Printed in the USA
LVOW07s1455160315

430764LV00020B/1120/P

9 780573 60934